Science
CHEMISTRY

FOR COMMON ENTRANCE

Ron Pickering

GALORE PARK

AN HACHETTE UK COMPANY

The publishers would like to thank the following for permission to reproduce copyright material:

Photo credits

b = bottom, m = middle, t = top, r = right, l = left

Cover photo © Marcin Chodorowski/Fotolia **pvii** © Tyler Olson/Fotolia **px** © Mike/Fotolia **pxi** © Dusan Kostic/Fotolia **pxxv**r © Science Photo Library/Charles D. Winters **p18** © Pictorial Press Ltd/Alamy **p19**tl © Africa Studio/Fotolia **p19**tr © Ruslan Grumble/Fotolia **p19**mtr © andreistanciulescu/Fotolia **p19**mr © Getty Images/iStockphoto/Thinkstock **p19**mbr © Getty Images/iStockphoto/Thinkstock **p19**bl © Getty Images/iStockphoto/Thinkstock **p19**br © Brian Jackson/Fotolia **p21**tl © Charles D. Winters/Science Photo Library **p21**tm © tiero/Fotolia **p21**tr © Andrew McClenaghan/Science Photo Library **p21**bl © Andrew Lambert Photography/Science Photo Library **p21**bm © Martyn F Chillmaid/Science Photo Library **p21**br © Andrew Lambert Photography/Science Photo Library **p22** © Getty Images/iStockphoto/Thinkstock **p36**t © GIPhotoStock/Science Photo Library **p36**m © GIPhotoStock/Science Photo Library **p36**b © GIPhotoStock/Science Photo Library **p48** © david pearson/Alamy **p64**l © York/Fotolia **p64**br © BernardBreton/Fotolia **p65** © Photographee.eu/Fotolia **p68** © Bruce Adams/Daily Mail/ REX **p73** © krishnacreations/Fotolia **p74** © Saidin Jusoh/Fotolia **p87** © Getty Images/iStockphoto/Thinkstock **p93** © Andrew Lambert Photography/Science Photo Library **p96** © taweepat/Fotolia **p110**l © Martyn F. Chillmaid/Science Photo Library **p120**t © Getty Images/iStockphoto/Thinkstock **p120**b © Getty Images/iStockphoto/Thinkstock

pxxiv, pxxvl, **p62, p64**tr, **p99, p100, p110**r, **p118**b, **p118**t and **p121** © **Ron Pickering**

Every effort has been made to trace all copyright holders, but if any have been inadvertently overlooked the publishers will be pleased to make the necessary arrangements at the first opportunity.

Although every effort has been made to ensure that website addresses are correct at time of going to press, Galore Park cannot be held responsible for the content of any website mentioned in this book. It is sometimes possible to find a relocated web page by typing in the address of the home page for a website in the URL window of your browser.

Hachette UK's policy is to use papers that are natural, renewable and recyclable products and made from wood grown in sustainable forests. The logging and manufacturing processes are expected to conform to the environmental regulations of the country of origin.

Orders: please contact Bookpoint Ltd, 130 Milton Park, Abingdon, Oxon OX14 4SB. Telephone: +44 (0)1235 827827. Lines are open 9.00a.m.–5.00p.m., Monday to Saturday, with a 24-hour message answering service. Visit our website at www.galorepark.co.uk for details of other revision guides for Common Entrance, examination papers and Galore Park publications.

Published by Galore Park Publishing Ltd

An Hachette UK company

Carmelite House, 50 Victoria Embankment, London, EC4Y 0DZ

www.galorepark.co.uk

Text copyright © Ron Pickering 2015

Typeset in 11.5/13 ITC Officina Sans/Book by Integra Software Services Pvt. Ltd, Pondicherry, India.

Printed in India

New illustrations by Integra Software Services Pvt. Ltd, Pondicherry, India except page xxiii by Barking Dog Art, UK.

Some illustrations by Graham Edwards were re-used. The publishers will be pleased to make the necessary arrangements with regard to these illustrations at the first opportunity.

A catalogue record for this title is available from the British Library.

ISBN: 9781471847103

About the author

Ron Pickering has published a number of very successful books covering the GCSE, IGCSE and A level syllabi and has worked in both maintained and independent education for more than 30 years. He now divides his time between teacher training, both in the UK and overseas, and writing, and has been a science advisor and curriculum manager at Altrincham Grammar School for Girls, as well as a Science Inspector for OFSTED.

Ron extends his interest in science by spending many hours photographing animals, both in the wild and in captive environments, and tries to maintain some level of fitness by off-road cycling.

Dedication

I dedicate this book to all young scientists, wherever they are, but especially to two microscientists, Noah and Kay, our beloved grandsons.

- Ron Pickering

Contents

Introduction

○ About this book

Science for Common Entrance: Chemistry covers the Chemistry component of Science at Key Stage 3 and is part of an ISEB-approved course leading to 13+ Common Entrance.

In this book you will learn about the properties of different materials. You will see that many of these properties are explained by the fact that all materials are made up of tiny particles, called atoms. Understanding the properties of materials will enable you to predict how materials will react with one another.

This book is part of a *Science for Common Entrance* series, which also includes *Biology* and *Physics*.

- *Biology*: In this book you will continue your exploration and investigations into the lives of plants and animals. You will learn something about the ways in which different living organisms, including ourselves, all depend on one another for survival; about how different organisms get their differences, and how they are passed on from generation to generation.
- *Physics*: In this book you will study the physical processes that affect your everyday life. The book will explain about forces, electricity and magnetism, and the properties of light rays and sound waves.

Of course, scientists from the different areas of science work together so don't be surprised if you are asked to think about some Biology as you study Chemistry, or some Chemistry as you study Physics!

What do we mean by science?

As you go through these books you will continue to build on the scientific knowledge you have already gained. Remember that asking questions about the world around you is the first step to becoming a scientist. Carrying out experiments is a good way for scientists to start finding things out and to begin to answer some of the more challenging questions we have. You will already have got to grips with the idea of conducting fair tests when carrying out experiments, and in this book we will give you the opportunity to do many more. You will also see some of the things we have found out from the results of experiments carried out by other scientists.

◯ Notes on features in this book

Words printed in **blue bold** are keywords. All keywords are defined in the Glossary at the end of the book.

Sometimes you will see the heading '**Preliminary knowledge**'. The material in these sections is a reminder of things you should have learned at primary school. If any of this material is not familiar take time to ask your teacher or read about the subject in books or online before moving on.

> Useful rules and reminders and additional notes, looking like this, are scattered throughout the book.

> **Did you know?**
>
> In these boxes you will learn interesting and often surprising facts about the natural world to inform your understanding of each topic. Sometimes you will find a brief biography of an important scientist. You are **not** expected to learn these facts for your exam.

Working scientifically is an important part of learning science. When you see this heading you will be reading about the skills and attitudes you need to become a good scientist. You will find out:

| Working Scientifically

- why we carry out experiments
- how to plan and carry out experiments
- how to evaluate risks
- how we ensure our findings are accurate and precise
- what we mean by the word 'variable'
- how to identify the independent, dependent and control variables
- how we measure variables
- what we mean by a fair test
- how to properly record and display results and observations
- how to spot patterns and draw conclusions
- how to calculate results, analyse data and use simple statistical techniques
- how scientific methods and theories develop as scientists modify explanations to take into account new evidence and ideas
- about the power and limitations of science and potential ethical issues.

Investigation

When we think like a scientist we might try to give some sort of explanation for what we observe. For example, we might think that some mice are bigger than others because of what they eat.

In an investigation you will see a brief overview of how to carry out an experiment and how to record and interpret your observations in order to check out an explanation. Sometimes sample data is provided so that you can practise data analysis techniques, presenting data in graphs and charts and interpreting results and drawing conclusions.

The investigations given in this book are **not** intended as step-by-step instructions – your teacher or technician should provide these and carry out their own risk assessment if you are to carry out the investigation in the classroom. Do **not** try any of these investigations outside of the classroom without teacher supervision.

Exercise

Exercises of varying lengths are provided to give you plenty of opportunities to practise what you have learned. Answers are provided in the separate resource, *Science for Common Entrance: Chemistry Answers*.

Go further

When you see this heading, this highlights information that is beyond the requirements of the ISEB 13+ Common Entrance exam. You therefore do not need to remember the detail of this information for your exam, but it is helpful to understand the principles and applications of science described, in order to fully support your understanding of the subject area.

What is chemistry?

For many people, a first contact with chemistry involves watching films or cartoons showing strange scientists messing about with bubbling liquids, smelly gases, loud explosions and bright flashes. These things can be explained by chemistry, but the subject involves a lot more.

In the simplest terms, **chemistry is the study of materials**. Chemists study the physical properties of different substances and they also try to understand the reactions between different substances. Everything in our world is made of materials – all these materials are chemicals. Chemicals are found in chemistry laboratories, but you are far more likely to come across them in your food, in detergents, medicines, cosmetics, in your car, your clothes or in the decoration in your bedroom. The air you breathe is made up of chemicals and so is your body.

Chemistry has helped us to explain how one substance can be changed into another. These changes, called chemical reactions, occur all around us. They include:

- the burning of fuels
- the cooking of foods
- the rusting of cars and bicycles
- the breakdown of household waste
- the growth of plants and animals.

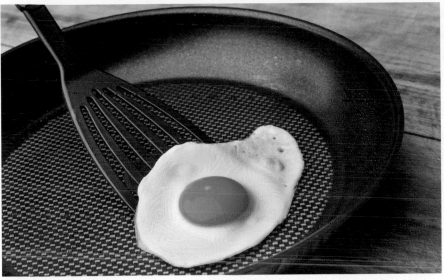

■ Cooking your breakfast involves a chemical reaction

The study of chemical reactions, especially finding out the most efficient way of making new substances, is the basis of the chemical industry. Understanding chemistry helps us to make the best use of our environment while limiting the damage we cause. An important example studied later in this book is the efficient extraction of metals from the Earth.

There are several important branches of the chemical industry:

- The petrochemical industry uses oil as a raw material to produce fuels, plastics and building materials.
- The pharmaceutical industry uses many different raw materials to produce drugs and medicines for the treatment of disease and the relief of pain, and hormones to increase the growth of animals and plants.
- The agrochemical industry produces pesticides, fertilisers and other products required for farming.

Many important advances in science, medicine and technology have been made possible by the production of new chemicals. Silicon chips in computers, drugs for helping asthma sufferers and super-strong alloys in racing cars would not exist without the efforts of chemists. Nowadays many chemists are involved with caring for the environment. We are beginning to understand how to recycle many of the materials we have developed for our use. Everyone can benefit from the study of chemistry.

Investigations in science

Before we launch into this book it is worth pausing and taking time to go over some of the rules we need to follow in order that we can carry out experiments in a reliable way. These rules apply whether you are studying biology, chemistry or physics.

What is an experiment?

Every day we make hundreds of observations; for example, 'more sugar dissolves in warm water', 'that car is moving faster than the other one', 'that sunflower is taller than the one next to it' or 'some of the pet mice are bigger than the others'.

When we think like a scientist we might try to give an explanation for some of these observations. We might think that some mice are bigger than others because of what they eat. We might think that one sunflower is taller than the one next to it because it is getting more sunshine. Before it is proven, we call this explanation a **hypothesis**.

An **experiment** is a way of collecting information to see whether our hypothesis is correct. Before a scientist begins an experiment, he or she will have a definite **purpose** or **aim**. The aim of an experiment is a way of stating carefully what you are trying to find out. For example, 'My aim is to investigate the effect of temperature on the amount of sugar that dissolves in water'. Not just, 'Study sugar dissolving in water'.

What about variables?

An experiment has the aim of investigating the effect of one factor (temperature, for example) on another factor (such as mass of sugar that dissolves). These factors can have different values and so are called variables. In our experiment we can change the **values** of these variables, so we might make one sugar solution using warmer water than another. Anything that we can measure is a variable.

The experiment must be a fair test

Here are the steps you should follow before conducting an experiment:

Step 1: Write down your hypothesis and identify the variables. (Variables are factors that might affect the results.)

Step 2: Choose which variable you will change. This is called the **independent (input) variable**.

Step 3: Choose the variable that you think will be affected by changing the independent (input) variable. This is called the **dependent (outcome) variable**.

Step 4: Decide what equipment you will need to measure any changes. Then go ahead and carry out your experiment.

You are trying to find out whether the change in the independent variable causes a change in the dependent variable.

An experiment will not be a **fair test** if you change more than one variable at a time. To make sure that the experiment is a fair test, you will need to check that none of the other possible variables is changing.

For example, in the experiment investigating the dissolving of sugar in water, it is possible that the mass that dissolves might be affected by any of the following factors:

- how big the granules of sugar are
- how much water is used to dissolve the sugar
- how many times the solution is stirred
- the temperature of the water
- how big the glass beaker is.

These are the variables. If you want to investigate how temperature affects the amount of sugar that dissolves in water, temperature would be your independent (input) variable and you would change its value. All of the other variables **must stay the same**. These are called the **control variables**.

Finally remember to **work safely**.

- Always wash your hands after touching plants or animals.
- Carry equipment carefully.
- Don't run in the laboratory.
- Wear suitable clothing.

How we measure variables

Scientists often need special equipment to measure any changes in variables during the course of their experiments. Some of these pieces of equipment, and what you would use them for, are described here.

Measuring length using a ruler

A ruler can be made of wood, metal or plastic. Along the length of the ruler is a numbered scale. One of the benefits of a plastic ruler is that it is usually transparent, so the object to be measured can be seen through it. The following diagram reminds you how to use a ruler.

> Make sure the scale is right next to the object you are trying to measure.

> The plastic is transparent and enables you to see the object through the plastic, if it is underneath, and helps you to line up the ruler properly.

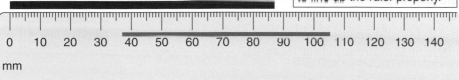

> Try to get the object up against the 0 on the ruler.

> 1) How long is the red line in millimetres (mm)?
> 2) How long is the blue line in millimetres (mm)?

Measuring volume using a beaker or a measuring cylinder

Beakers and **measuring cylinders** can be made out of glass or plastic. Scientists now often use plastic because it is less likely to break and so is safer. However, plastic beakers can't be used to boil liquids because they would melt and become distorted and useless.

The following diagram shows you how to use a measuring cylinder and a beaker.

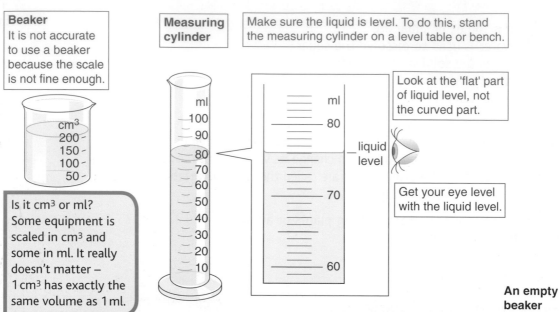

Beaker
It is not accurate to use a beaker because the scale is not fine enough.

Measuring cylinder

Make sure the liquid is level. To do this, stand the measuring cylinder on a level table or bench.

Look at the 'flat' part of liquid level, not the curved part.

liquid level

Get your eye level with the liquid level.

Is it cm³ or ml? Some equipment is scaled in cm³ and some in ml. It really doesn't matter – 1 cm³ has exactly the same volume as 1 ml.

Measuring other things

There are other things that scientists want to measure. These include temperature, force and mass. Measuring force is described in Physics, Chapter 3.

Measuring mass using a balance

Mass is the name given by scientists to the amount of a substance. You can use a **balance** (also called a **weighing machine** or **scales**) to measure the mass of something. It is very important to remember that if you are weighing liquid in a container, you must subtract the mass of the container. You can do this as follows:

Step 1: Weigh the empty beaker. Note down its mass.
Step 2: Add the liquid and weigh the beaker again. Note down this mass.
Step 3: Subtract the mass of the empty beaker (Step 1) from the mass of the beaker containing liquid (Step 2).

An empty beaker

Balance (weighing machine)

The beaker containing liquid

Measuring temperature using a thermometer

'Heat' is one kind of energy. If a material has a lot of heat (or thermal energy) we say it is **hot**, and if it has very little heat (thermal energy) we say it is **cold**. **Temperature** is a scale of numbers that we use to measure the amount of thermal energy that a material has.

We measure temperature using an instrument called a **thermometer**. There are many different kinds of thermometer, but there is one type that you will often see in a school laboratory. This kind of thermometer has mercury or a coloured liquid inside a very thin tube; as the liquid gets hotter it **expands** (gets bigger) and as it gets cooler it **contracts** (gets smaller). The length of the coloured liquid against a scale gives us the measure of how hot it is. This way of measuring temperature is shown in the following diagram.

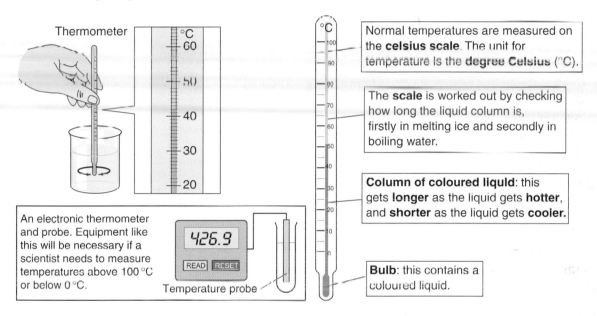

Thermometer

Normal temperatures are measured on the **celsius scale**. The unit for temperature is the **degree Celsius** (°C).

The **scale** is worked out by checking how long the liquid column is, firstly in melting ice and secondly in boiling water.

Column of coloured liquid: this gets **longer** as the liquid gets **hotter**, and **shorter** as the liquid gets **cooler**.

An electronic thermometer and probe. Equipment like this will be necessary if a scientist needs to measure temperatures above 100 °C or below 0 °C.

Temperature probe

Bulb: this contains a coloured liquid.

When people make thermometers, the first thing they have to do is devise a scale. They start by defining 0 °C as the temperature of melting ice and 100 °C as the temperature of boiling water. Once they know where 0 °C and 100 °C are, by dipping the thermometer in melting ice and then in boiling water, they then divide up the space between the two points to make a scale.

This table gives you a summary of different types of measuring equipment and their uses:

■ Measuring equipment for use in science

Equipment	What it measures	Units (symbol)
Forcemeter	Force (and weight)	Newtons (N)
Stopwatch or stopclock (analogue or digital)	Time	Seconds (s) and minutes (min) 60 s = 1 min
Measuring cylinder or beaker	Volume	Millilitres (ml) and litres (l) 1000 ml = 1 l
Balance (usually electronic pan balances)	Mass	Grams (g) and kilograms (kg) 1000 g = 1 kg
Ruler/tape measure	Length	Millimetres (mm) and metres (m) 1000 mm = 1 m
Thermometer	Temperature	Degrees Celsius (°C)

Exercise 1: Made to measure

Measuring cylinders and beakers are made from either glass or plastic.

1 Give two reasons why glass and plastic are useful materials.
2 Give one reason why glass is more useful than plastic when making measuring equipment.
3 Give one reason why plastic is more useful than glass when making measuring equipment.

Extension questions

4 Look at these diagrams.

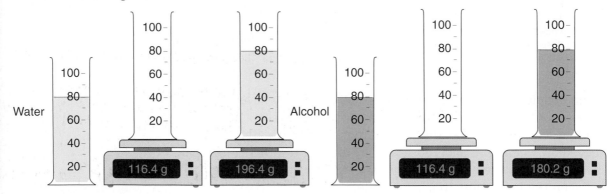

A scientist has measured the mass and the volume of some water and some alcohol. What can you tell from the measurements?

5 Minnie is going on a four-hour journey and she wants to take some water. She has a water container that weighs 120 g. She doesn't want to carry more than 260 g altogether. She would normally drink about 200 ml in four hours.
   (a) What is the maximum mass of water she should take with her?
   (b) What volume of water will this be? Will she have enough for her journey?
        Hint: 1 ml of water weighs 1 g.

Making a record of our results

Results (or **observations**) are a record of the measurements you have taken during an experiment. There are certain rules about the way you should show these results. They should be recorded in a table, like the one shown below.

Making a table of results

Give the columns headings by putting the name of the variable **and** the units.

In the first (left-hand) column, put the values for the **independent variable**, e.g. the temperature of the water.

Write the values as **decimals** not as **fractions**, e.g. 6.5 not 6½.

Temperature of water, in °C	Mass of sugar that dissolves in 100 ml of water, in grams			Average mass of dissolved sugar in grams
	Test 1	Test 2	Test 3	
0	152	150	148	150
10	165	167	163	165
20	183	183	180	182
30	201	200	199	200
50	261	266	268	265
70	365	364	366	365
80	421	426	428	425
90	478	471	476	475

Use a ruler to draw lines around your table. It makes it look **neater** and **more scientific!**

In the right-hand columns, put the values for the **dependent variable**, e.g. mass of sugar that dissolves for each test.

Calculate the mean (average) and put this in the last column.

Put the numbers in order, not just mixed up. If you do, it makes it much easier to see patterns in your results.

When you look at your results, you may see a certain pattern. It might seem, for example, that the higher the temperature, the more sugar dissolves.

Your results will be more reliable if you carry out each test more than once and then take an **average** (mean) of the results. This will remove any unusual results from, for example, inaccurate measurements of mass or volume.

The mean is calculated by adding together all your results and dividing by the number of repeats. For example, the mean of 152, 150 and 148 is:

$$\frac{(152 + 150 + 148)}{3} = 150$$

If one or two of the results don't fit the pattern, the first thing to do is check your measurement. If your measurement was accurate, and you have the time, you can **repeat** the test to check the 'odd' result.

Displaying your results

Sometimes you can see a pattern in your results from the table you have made, but this is not always the case. It often helps to present your results in a different way. **Charts** and **graphs** display your results like pictures and they can make it very easy to see patterns, but only if they are drawn in the correct way. There are rules for drawing graphs and charts, just as there are rules for putting results into tables.

- First of all, look at the variables you measured. If both of the variables have numbers as their values, you should draw (sometimes we say 'plot') a **line graph**. If one of the variables isn't measured in numbers, you should choose a **bar chart**.
- You should always put the **independent (input) variable** on the horizontal (*x*) axis and the **dependent (outcome) variable** on the vertical (*y*) axis. If you don't do this, you can easily mix up the patterns between the two variables.

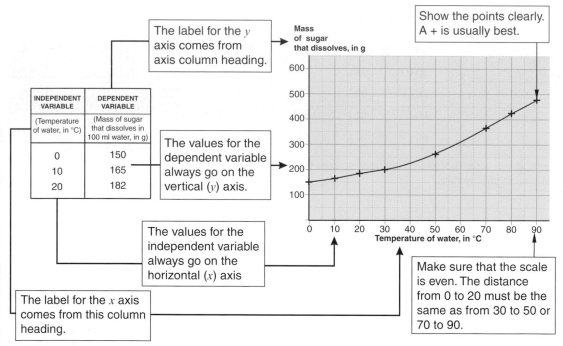

How to draw a line graph

The title should be 'The effect of temperature on the mass of sugar that will dissolve in 100 ml of water'. The simple rule is: 'Effect of (independent variable) on (dependent variable)'.

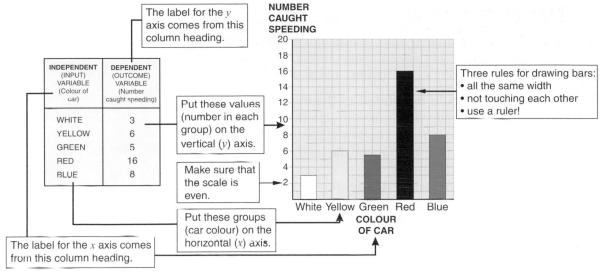

The label for the y axis comes from this column heading.

INDEPENDENT (INPUT) VARIABLE (Colour of car)	DEPENDENT (OUTCOME) VARIABLE (Number caught speeding)
WHITE	3
YELLOW	6
GREEN	5
RED	16
BLUE	8

Put these values (number in each group) on the vertical (y) axis.

Make sure that the scale is even.

Put these groups (car colour) on the horizontal (x) axis.

The label for the x axis comes from this column heading.

Three rules for drawing bars:
• all the same width
• not touching each other
• use a ruler!

■ How to draw a bar chart

In this case the title should be 'The effect of the colour of the car on the number caught speeding.'

Using graphs

A graph can let you see a pattern between two variables. For example, as temperature increases, so does the solubility of the sugar. The graph can also let you make **predictions** if it shows an obvious pattern. So, you might be able to predict how much sugar would dissolve at a particular temperature.

Just before we look at how to do this using a graph, it is worth making an important point about predictions. It can be very useful indeed to make some of your own predictions even before you get started on your experiment. If you do this, it can help you to plan much better experiments. If we take the example of looking at the effect temperature has on the solubility of sugar, we can make a pretty good guess (a prediction) that the higher the temperature, the more sugar will dissolve. We can also start to plan what apparatus we will need and so on.

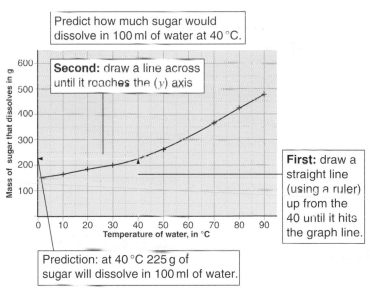

Predict how much sugar would dissolve in 100 ml of water at 40 °C.

Second: draw a line across until it reaches the (y) axis

First: draw a straight line (using a ruler) up from the 40 until it hits the graph line.

Prediction: at 40 °C 225 g of sugar will dissolve in 100 ml of water.

Making conclusions

Once you have collected all of your results into a table, and perhaps drawn a graph or chart, you need to sum up what you have found out. This summing up is called a **conclusion**, and here are some tips:

- **Your conclusion should be related to the aim of your experiment.** If your aim was to investigate the effect of light intensity on plant growth and you saw a clear pattern, then your conclusion might be that 'the higher the light intensity, the taller the plant'.
- **Try to write your conclusion simply.** One sentence is often enough, but make sure it explains how the independent (input) variable affects the dependent (outcome) variable for your experiment.
- **Don't just describe your results.** For example, in the experiment on dissolving sugar, the statement 'a high temperature makes more sugar dissolve' is really giving only one of your results. A much better conclusion would be 'the higher the temperature, the greater the mass of sugar that will dissolve in water'.

◯ Experiments in chemistry: important apparatus and skills

Chemistry is a practical subject. The laws of chemistry have been worked out by scientists who have carried out experiments to test their ideas. The results collected by these scientists will only be acceptable if:

- they have designed their experiments carefully
- they have been able to use the correct apparatus
- they have been able to measure variables accurately
- their results can be repeated by other scientists.

Apparatus

Apparatus is the name we give to the equipment used in a science laboratory. A diagram of apparatus is often very useful when a chemist has to describe an experiment. Each piece of apparatus can be drawn in an outline form. An outline diagram is quick to produce and should be clear to any other user.

Throughout this book you will see both 3-D pictures of apparatus and scientific drawings. It is very important that you learn how to draw apparatus correctly otherwise you may be drawing experiments that wouldn't work at all or that may even be dangerous. The table below shows the 3-D pictures and the way you must draw these pieces of apparatus.

Each piece of apparatus has a particular function.

3-D picture	Description	Scientific drawing
	● **Conical flask:** used for mixing solutions, without heating.	
	● **Watch glass:** used for collecting and evaporating liquids without heating (see 'Separating solids and water: evaporation and crystallisation' in Chapter 5).	
	● **Gas jar:** to collect gases for testing.	
	● **Filter funnel:** used to separate solids from liquids, using filter paper (see 'Separating a solid from a liquid: filtration' in Chapter 4).	
	● **Measuring cylinder:** used for measuring the volume of liquids (see 'Measuring volume using a beaker or a measuring cylinder' earlier in this Introduction).	

3-D picture	Description	Scientific drawing
	● **Thermometer:** used to measure temperature (see 'Measuring temperature using a thermometer' earlier in this Introduction).	
	● **Spatula:** used for handling solid chemicals; for example, when adding a solid to a liquid.	
	● **Pipette:** used to measure and transfer small volumes of liquids (see 'Universal indicator and the pH scale' in Chapter 9).	
	● **Stand, boss and clamp:** used to support the apparatus in place. This reduces the risk of dangerous spills. This is not generally drawn. If the clamp is merely to support a piece of apparatus, it is usually represented by two crosses as shown.	
	● **Bunsen burner:** used to heat the contents of other apparatus (e.g. a liquid in a test tube) or for directly heating solids (see diagram in Exercise 7.3: Conservation of mass).	THERMAL ENERGY
	● **Tripod:** used to support apparatus above a Bunsen burner. The Bunsen burner, tripod and gauze are the most common way of heating materials in school science laboratories.	
	● **Gauze:** used to spread out the thermal energy from a Bunsen burner and to support the apparatus on a tripod.	- - - - -
	● **Test tube and boiling tube:** used for heating solids and liquids. They are also used to hold chemicals while other substances are added and mixed (see 'Using litmus' in Chapter 9). They need to be put safely in a test tube rack.	
	● **Evaporating dish:** used to collect and evaporate liquids with or without heating (see 'Chemical reactions can be reversed' in Chapter 7).	
	● **Beaker:** used for mixing solutions and for heating liquids (see 'Making salts' in Chapter 9).	
	● **Round bottom flask:** used for heating liquids: for example, during distillation (see 'Separation of a solvent from a solution: simple distillation' in Chapter 5).	
	● **Flat bottom flask:** used for mixing liquids. It should not be heated strongly or it may crack.	

Investigations in science

The other very important measuring device in the laboratory is a balance (weighing machine) see page xiv.

Chemicals

Doing experiments in chemistry often involves making changes to materials. We often call the materials we use in experiments chemicals. It is extremely important that these chemicals are used safely. Some chemicals are too dangerous to be used in school laboratories and all of them must be used with great care.

Hazard symbols

To help us identify which chemicals are particularly dangerous, we have a series of hazard symbols that appear on containers holding chemicals. These symbols warn us of special dangers and they also help teachers and technicians decide on the best thing to do if a chemical is spilled or swallowed by mistake. These symbols, and some examples of the chemicals that are marked with them, are shown in the following table.

Hazard symbols

Symbol	Description	Examples	Symbol	Description	Examples
	Oxidising These substances provide oxygen, which allows other materials to burn more fiercely.	Bleach, sodium chlorate, potassium nitrate		**Harmful** These substances are similar to toxic substances but less dangerous	Dilute acids and alkalis
	Highly flammable These substances easily catch fire.	Ethanol, petrol, acetone		**Corrosive** These substances attack and destroy living tissues,including eyes and skin.	Concentrated acids and alkalis
	Toxic These substances can cause death. They may have their effects when swallowed or breathed in or absorbed through the skin.	Mercury, copper sulfate		**Irritant** These substances are not corrosive but can cause reddening or blistering of the skin.	Ammonia, dilute acids and alkalis

Some chemicals can have more than one label. For example, petrol is:

- flammable
- harmful
- an irritant!

Lab safety rules:

- Always wear eye protection when handling or heating chemicals.
- Wear a long-sleeved overall to protect clothes and skin if handling corrosive materials.
- Tie back long hair.

Exercise 2: Experiments in chemistry

1 Briefly describe what each of the following pieces of apparatus is used for:
   - (a) conical flask
   - (b) tripod
   - (c) measuring cylinder
   - (d) filter funnel
   - (e) spatula
   - (f) pipette.

2 Make the following conversions of units:
   - (a) 1.22 kg to g
   - (b) 4 min 19 s to s
   - (c) 1320 s to minutes and seconds
   - (d) 2340 cm^3 to litres
   - (e) 3400 g to kg
   - (f) 2984 cm^3 to ml

Extension question

3 Identify the potential hazards of working in this laboratory. How many of them can you identify? What advice would you give to prevent them?

Using a Bunsen burner

Chemical reactions always involve an energy change. Some chemical reactions are **exothermic** (give out thermal energy) and some are **endothermic** (take in thermal energy).

Chemical reactions often require some form of heating. Even reactions that are exothermic (give out thermal energy) may need some thermal energy to get them started. A good example of this kind of reaction is using a match. The match gives out energy when it burns, but won't even start to burn until some thermal energy is provided by friction when the match is struck against a rough surface.

Experiments in the laboratory often need some type of heating. This heating must be reliable (you can get it whenever you need it) and it must be controllable (you can vary the amount of thermal energy). The **Bunsen burner** is the most common source of thermal energy used in the laboratory. It is safe and easy to use, but the user needs to stick to some rules!

- Always wear eye protection.
- Keep long hair tied back and loose clothing (such as ties) tucked in.
- Have a **flame** ready to light the Bunsen burner before turning on the **gas supply**.
- Check that the **air hole** is closed before turning on the gas supply and lighting the Bunsen burner.
- When you are not using the Bunsen burner, either turn it off or close the air hole to give a **yellow** flame. The yellow flame is **luminous** so that it can be seen easily. This means that there is less risk of someone accidentally being burned.
- Never leave a lit Bunsen burner unattended.
- For gentle heating, half open the air hole to give a **quiet blue** flame.
- For strong heating, have the air hole wide open. This will give a **roaring blue** flame.

Remember: when you are drawing a scientific diagram, the symbol for a Bunsen burner is:

THERMAL ENERGY

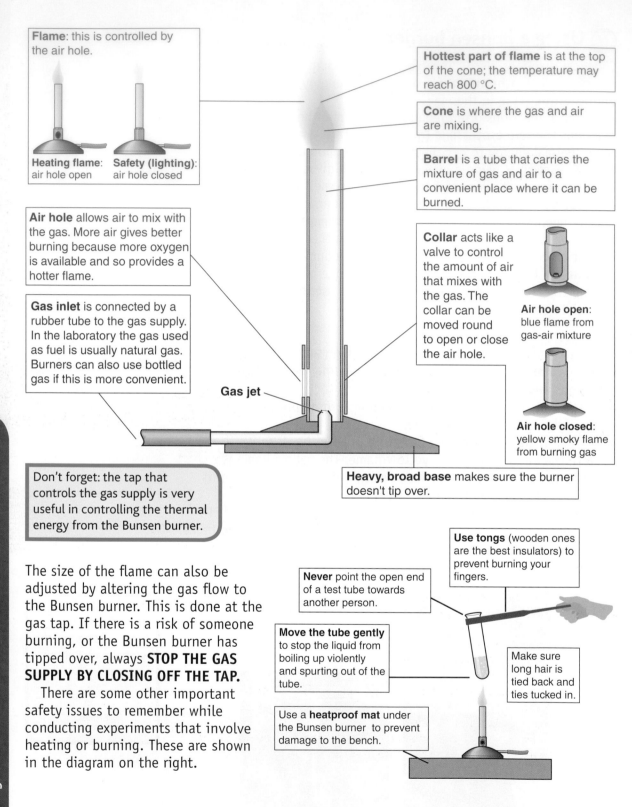

Flame: this is controlled by the air hole.

Heating flame: air hole open

Safety (lighting): air hole closed

Hottest part of flame is at the top of the cone; the temperature may reach 800 °C.

Cone is where the gas and air are mixing.

Barrel is a tube that carries the mixture of gas and air to a convenient place where it can be burned.

Air hole allows air to mix with the gas. More air gives better burning because more oxygen is available and so provides a hotter flame.

Gas inlet is connected by a rubber tube to the gas supply. In the laboratory the gas used as fuel is usually natural gas. Burners can also use bottled gas if this is more convenient.

Collar acts like a valve to control the amount of air that mixes with the gas. The collar can be moved round to open or close the air hole.

Air hole open: blue flame from gas-air mixture

Air hole closed: yellow smoky flame from burning gas

Gas jet

Heavy, broad base makes sure the burner doesn't tip over.

Don't forget: the tap that controls the gas supply is very useful in controlling the thermal energy from the Bunsen burner.

The size of the flame can also be adjusted by altering the gas flow to the Bunsen burner. This is done at the gas tap. If there is a risk of someone burning, or the Bunsen burner has tipped over, always **STOP THE GAS SUPPLY BY CLOSING OFF THE TAP.**

There are some other important safety issues to remember while conducting experiments that involve heating or burning. These are shown in the diagram on the right.

Use tongs (wooden ones are the best insulators) to prevent burning your fingers.

Never point the open end of a test tube towards another person.

Move the tube gently to stop the liquid from boiling up violently and spurting out of the tube.

Make sure long hair is tied back and ties tucked in.

Use a **heatproof mat** under the Bunsen burner to prevent damage to the bench.

Investigations in science

Exercise 3: The Bunsen burner

1 Lena and Louis were carrying out an experiment to find out whether a Bunsen burner delivers more thermal energy with the air hole open or with it closed. They were measuring the thermal energy from the Bunsen burner by finding out the time taken for some water to boil.

(a) What is the independent variable in this experiment?

(b) What is the dependent variable in this experiment?

(c) Lena and Louis knew that there should also be controlled variables, i.e. things that had to be kept constant for this to be a fair test. If any of these were changed, the outcome of the experiment could be affected. Which variables from the list below should be controlled?

(i) The size and shape of the beaker.

(ii) The starting temperature of the water.

(iii) Which day of the week they did the experiment.

(iv) The position of the Bunsen burner below the beaker.

(v) The position of the gas tap (how much flow of gas).

(vi) The volume of water in the beaker.

2 Sara carried out a series of experiments to investigate how much thermal energy could be produced by a Bunsen burner. She used a stopwatch to measure how long it took for some water in a beaker to boil. She altered some of the conditions from one experiment to the next. The results of her experiments are shown in the table.

Working Scientifically

Experiment	Volume of water/cm³	Temperature at start of heating/°C	Gas tap	Air hole in Bunsen burner	Time for water to boil/seconds
I	100	20	Fully on	Open	155
II	100	50	Fully on	Open	85
III	200	20	Half on	Open	275
IV	200	20	Half on	Closed	425
V	200	20	Fully on	Open	300

(a) Why is it not a fair test to compare the results for experiments II and III?

(b) (i) What is Sara testing when she compares results for experiments III and IV?

(ii) What conclusion can she come to? What does her conclusion allow her to deduce/hypothesise about having the air hole in the Bunsen burner open?

(c) (i) What is Sara testing when she compares results for experiments I and II?

(ii) What conclusion can she come to?

(d) Which results should Sara compare to find the effect of the volume of water on the time taken for the water to boil?

Useful chemical tests

During a chemical reaction new **products** are formed. The new product could be a solid, a liquid or a gas.

Testing for gases

Many gases are colourless, so we can't see them. We may be aware that a gas has been produced because we see some fizzing or a release of bubbles. If we get a colourless gas formed in a chemical reaction, we will need to use a test to find out what it is. Three gases that are commonly involved in chemical reactions are oxygen, carbon dioxide and hydrogen. There are simple tests for each of these gases:

Testing for carbon dioxide

For example:

calcium carbonate → calcium oxide + carbon dioxide

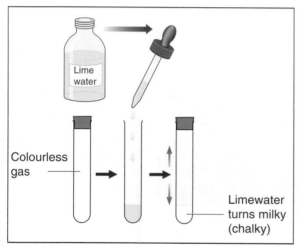

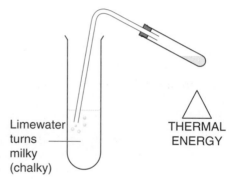

Testing for oxygen

For example:

potassium → potassium + manganese + oxygen
permanganate manganate oxide

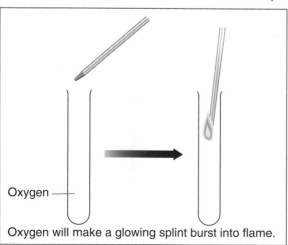

Oxygen will make a glowing splint burst into flame.

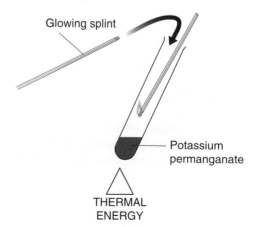

Investigations in science

Testing for hydrogen

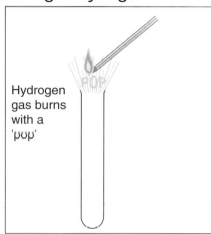

Hydrogen gas burns with a 'pop'

For example:

hydrochloric acid + zinc → zinc chloride + hydrogen

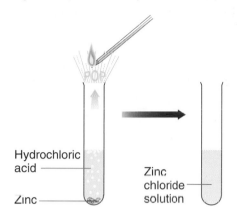

Hydrochloric acid

Zinc

Zinc chloride solution

Some gases are **coloured** (chlorine gas is green, for example) or they have a definite **smell** (hydrogen sulfide smells like rotten eggs). The smelly gases can be quite dangerous, and if there is any danger at all that a gas could be poisonous or an irritant, it should never be produced except in a fume cupboard (by a teacher). Some very dangerous gases, for example, carbon monoxide, are colourless and don't smell at all.

Testing for water

Many colourless liquids are **neutral**, which means they are neither acid nor alkali (see Chapter 9). Water is neutral along with many other clear liquids. To find out whether a clear liquid, produced during a chemical reaction, is in fact water, we can test it in one of two ways.

A useful and safe experiment to test for the presence of water uses anhydrous copper sulfate. This white powder turns blue in the presence of water.

Anhydrous copper sulfate is WHITE.   Copper sulfate is BLUE.

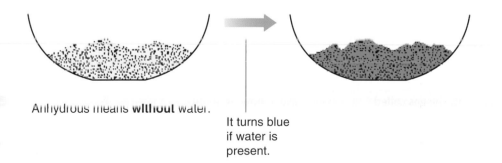

Anhydrous means **without** water.

It turns blue if water is present.

Another way of identifying water is to test it with blue **cobalt chloride** paper:

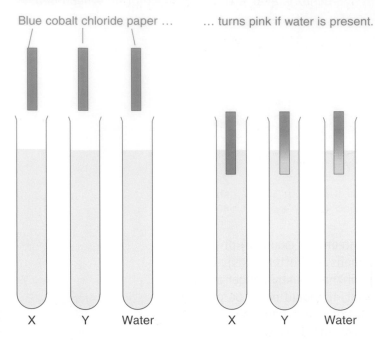

Blue cobalt chloride paper …   … turns pink if water is present.

X   Y   Water   X   Y   Water

Some crystals can remove water from the air. This can be useful. For example, silica gel crystals can keep water out of the air around delicate electronic equipment.

X is definitely not water.
Y contains water. You would need to carry out further tests to see if it is pure, such as:

- does it boil at 100 °C
- is it pH neutral?

Exercise 4: Testing

1 A chemical reaction gives out a vapour that can be cooled to give a colourless liquid.
   (a) Name two tests that could help you to decide whether this liquid is water.
   (b) What would the results be if the liquid were water?

2 Complete this paragraph, using words from the list below:

   carbon dioxide, relight, pop, milky, hydrogen, oxygen

   Limewater can be used to test for _____. The limewater will turn _____
   if carbon dioxide is present. The gas called _____ will make a glowing splint
   _____. A lighted splint will make the gas called _____ produce a sound like
   a _____.

1 Particle theory and states of matter

Preliminary knowledge: States of matter

All the materials on Earth can be placed into three groups: **solids**, **liquids** and **gases**.

These three different groups of materials have different properties that can affect the jobs they are used for. The most important properties are:

Can the material **flow**? Gases and liquids flow, but solids do not.

Can the material **change shape**? Solids keep the same shape, liquids change shape to match the shape of the container they are in, and gases spread out to fill any space they can reach. We can change the shape of a solid, but only by getting rid of some of it or by bending it.

Can the material be squeezed to **change its volume**? (In other words, can it be compressed?) It is easy to change the volume of a gas by squashing it. But liquids and solids do not tend to change very much in volume (although some can expand very, very slightly when heated).

Matter is the scientific word used to describe all of the different substances and materials found on the Earth (and in all other parts of the Universe). We call solid, liquid and gas the three states of matter.

Changing states

Here is some important information:

- Most substances can exist in all three states of matter.
- The state of a substance depends on the temperature.
- Changes of state are brought about by changes in temperature. Raising the temperature causes solids to change to liquids (**melting**) and, eventually, liquids to change to gases (**boiling** and **evaporation**). In the same way, cooling a gas will eventually change it into a liquid (**condensation**) and if the cooling is continued, the liquid will eventually change into a solid (**freezing**).

These changes of state are described in the diagram on the next page.

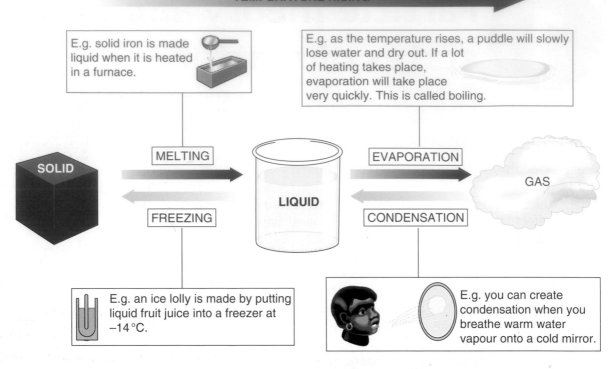

TEMPERATURE RISING

E.g. solid iron is made liquid when it is heated in a furnace.

E.g. as the temperature rises, a puddle will slowly lose water and dry out. If a lot of heating takes place, evaporation will take place very quickly. This is called boiling.

SOLID → MELTING → **LIQUID** → EVAPORATION → **GAS**

FREEZING ← CONDENSATION ←

E.g. an ice lolly is made by putting liquid fruit juice into a freezer at −14 °C.

E.g. you can create condensation when you breathe warm water vapour onto a cold mirror.

TEMPERATURE FALLING

In a **pure** substance these changes of state always occur at the same particular temperatures:

- the boiling point (bp)
- the melting point (mp)
- the freezing point (fp).

> You will learn the meaning of the word 'pure' in a chemical context in Chapter 3.

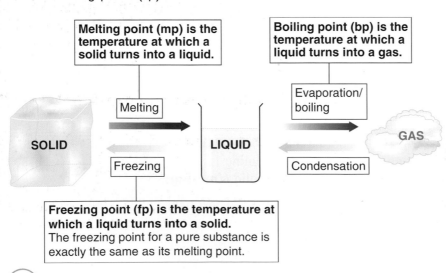

Melting point (mp) is the temperature at which a solid turns into a liquid.

Boiling point (bp) is the temperature at which a liquid turns into a gas.

SOLID → Melting → **LIQUID** → Evaporation/ boiling → **GAS**

Freezing ← Condensation ←

Freezing point (fp) is the temperature at which a liquid turns into a solid.
The freezing point for a pure substance is exactly the same as its melting point.

Did you know?
Pure water freezes at 0 °C but adding salt **lowers** the freezing point. That's why salt is spread on roads and paths in winter!

Every pure substance has its own particular melting point. Checking the melting point is one way to test how pure a substance is. A mixture of substances melts over a range of temperatures.

> Melting and boiling are described in more detail in the section on 'Particle theory and changes of state' later in this chapter.

A pure substance will also have its own particular boiling point. As we saw before, a mixture of substances would boil over a range of temperatures.

> **Did you know?**
>
> As you go up a mountain, the air pressure falls. At sea level water boils at 100 °C but it may boil at 70–80 °C up a mountain!

Because these temperatures are always the same for one particular substance, they can be counted as **properties** of the substance. Like other properties, they can help us to explain what a substance or material can be used for.

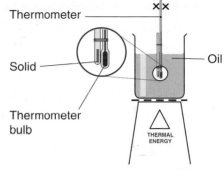

■ Finding the melting point of a solid

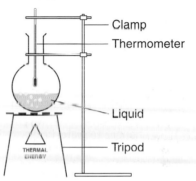

■ Finding the boiling point of a liquid

> Why does the water in an aluminium pan boil before the pan melts? As a result of its high melting point, aluminium has a useful property for pan making.

> Why is alcohol used as an antifreeze in car radiators?

■ Melting and boiling points of some common substances

Substance	Melting point/°C	Boiling point/°C
Oxygen	−219	−183
Mercury	−39	357
Water	0	100
Alcohol	−114	78
Aluminium	660	2467

Investigation: States of matter

The aim of this experiment is to observe and record what happens to various substances when they are heated.

Observe what happens when your teacher heats a test tube with some sulfur in it and then a test tube with some iodine in it.

Working Scientifically

Make a copy of the table below, then use it to describe what you saw happen.

Heat the other substances in clean test tubes; record what you observe in each case.

Some of these words may help:

melt, boil, freeze, gas, solid, liquid, condense, evaporate, solidify, sublime.

Work in groups and discuss your answers.

Substance	Observation
Iodine	
Sulfur	
Ice	
Wax	
Steric acid	

Safety: Iodine vapour is toxic. Take great care not to allow it to escape into the room.

1 You saw the substances in three different states. What were these?
2 Name the type of energy responsible for the changes of state you observed.
3 Name the change of state as:
   (a) ice changes to water
   (b) liquid water changes to water vapour.
4 Look at the diagram on page 12. Use this diagram to make simpler diagrams of what is happening to the particles of water when:
   (a) ice changes to water
   (b) liquid water changes to water vapour.

Other properties of solids, liquids and gases

There are several other important properties of substances that can help us to determine whether they are solids, liquids or gases.

Conduction of thermal (internal) energy

Solids that are metals are good at transferring thermal (internal) energy. We say they are good **conductors**.

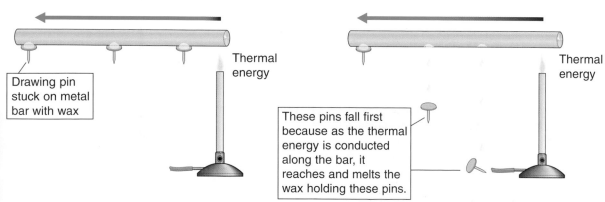

Drawing pin stuck on metal bar with wax

Thermal energy

These pins fall first because as the thermal energy is conducted along the bar, it reaches and melts the wax holding these pins.

Thermal energy

■ A demonstration of conduction along a metal bar

Liquids and gases are not good conductors. The only exception to this is mercury, which is a liquid *and* a metal and so does conduct.

Expansion

All states of matter **expand** when they are heated, but this is usually easier to see with solids. Gases expand more than liquids and liquids expand more than solids. When these materials are cooled again they usually **contract**.

When you put a thermometer under your tongue, the thermal energy makes the alcohol or mercury in the bulb of the thermometer expand and rise up the scale. This then gives a reading on the thermometer.

- In hot weather, the bridge sections expand.
- Gaps between the sections get smaller without damage.
- The rollers let the sections move as they expand.
- You will often see that the gaps in concrete roads are filled with tar. When the concrete expands, it just squashes the tar.

■ This bridge has been designed to prevent problems arising from expansion

Working Scientifically

Investigation: Heating and expansion

The aim of these experiments is to see what happens when certain substances are heated.

Heating a solid

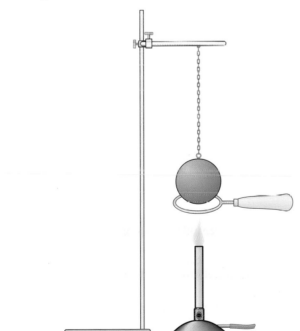

1 What is observed when the metal ball is heated?

Heating a liquid

2 What do you observe when the tube is warmed?

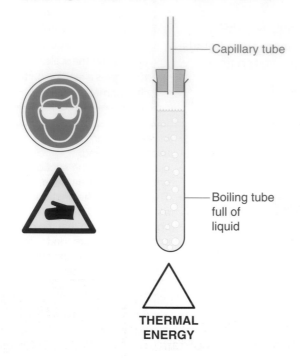

Capillary tube

Boiling tube
full of
liquid

THERMAL
ENERGY

Heating a gas

3 What happens when the flask of air is warmed gently by the hands?

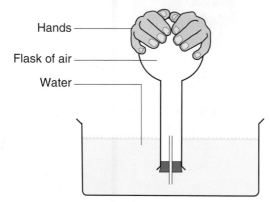

Hands

Flask of air

Water

4 Write down the words 'solids', 'liquids' and 'gases', in the order of which expands the most to which expands the least.

5 State what happens to the particles of a substance as the substance expands.

6 As a gas is warmed, the particles can move more easily and quickly. State the name of the 'energy of movement'.

Diffusion

All matter is made up of particles – you will learn more about this in the next section. Particles can spread out through liquids and gases, but not through solids. This spreading out is called **diffusion**. Diffusion is the result of the random movement of particles and the resulting collisions between them. This movement takes place as the particles absorb heat (thermal energy) and is called **Brownian motion**.

The particles spread out from where there are a lot of them (where they are **more concentrated**) to where there are fewer of them (where they are **less concentrated**). We say they move down a gradient of **concentration**. Diffusion goes on much more quickly if the temperature is raised.

The smell of fish and chips can spread out through the air. What we actually smell is particles from the fish and the fat and the ethanoic acid from the vinegar.

If you add concentrated orange squash to a glass of water you can observe diffusion as the whole glass of water turns orange.

What other examples of diffusion can you think of?

Diffusion takes place:

- when gases or liquids mix
- until the concentration of the two gases or liquids becomes the same everywhere.

Stretch and flow

Some substances can stretch or flow to fill a space. Solids do *not* stretch very easily, liquids can stretch and flow *quite* easily and most gases can flow *very* easily into new spaces.

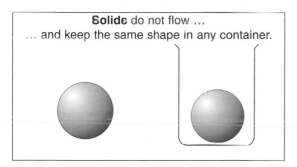

Solids do not flow ...
... and keep the same shape in any container.

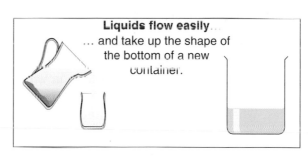

Liquids flow easily...
... and take up the shape of the bottom of a new container.

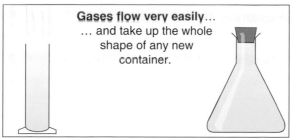

Gases flow very easily...
... and take up the whole shape of any new container.

Exercise 1.1: Solids, liquids and gases

1 Classify each of these materials as a solid, liquid or gas.

wood, carbon dioxide, snow, plastic, salt, vinegar, stone, lime juice, water vapour, tomato ketchup

2 Copy and complete this table about the properties of solids, liquids and gases.

Does it ...?	Solid	Liquid	Gas
Melt			
Freeze			
Boil			
Compress			
Conduct thermal energy			
Expand			
Diffuse			
Stretch			
Flow			

Particle theory and the properties of matter

All materials are made up of tiny particles called **atoms**. An atom is the basic unit that makes up a substance (although atoms themselves are made up of even smaller particles, as you will see in Chapter 2).

Some substances are made up of **molecules**. A molecule is made up of two or more atoms that are joined together. They can be atoms of the same type or groups of different atoms.

The atoms and molecules in matter can be arranged in different ways.

The theory about particles

Working Scientifically

Scientists have a theory that the way in which these particles are arranged helps to explain the different properties of solids, liquids and gases. Where did this **particle theory** come from? You will need to think back to how you would design an experiment or investigation.

Any theory about the nature of matter must be able to explain our observations (in other words, what we actually see happening to solids, liquids and gases). A theory is an idea that explains observations and these observations are the results obtained by carrying out experiments. The following flow diagram shows how a theory can be developed.

Creating a scientific theory

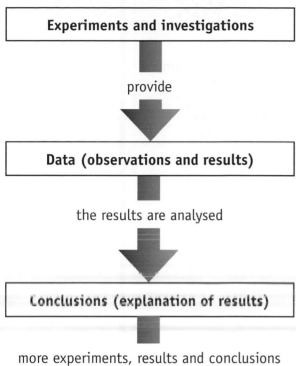

| Experiments and investigations |

provide

The data may come from using an instrument to make a measurement or to record some information.

| Data (observations and results) |

the results are analysed

| Conclusions (explanation of results) |

more experiments, results and conclusions

A theory may be altered many times as new experiments provide more results and observations.

| THEORY |

The way in which the particle theory can help to explain our observations on the properties of solids, liquids and gases is explained in the diagram on the next page.

The particle theory states the following:

- All solids, liquids and gases are made up of **very small particles**.
- Particles are **always moving** and have **spaces between them**.
- Particles are **held together by forces**.

Observations on the **properties** of solids, liquids and gases ...

Vibrations move along and conduct thermal energy.

Thermal energy

Conduction (internal/ thermal energy transfer). The particles in the solid must be close together to allow the energy to be passed from one particle to another along the bar.

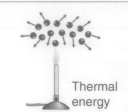

Thermal energy

Expansion (getting bigger on heating). The particles must move further apart from each other when they are heated as they have more energy. This could explain why the material **expands.**

... create ...

Density (how heavy something is for its size). Very **dense** materials (like metals) must have a lot of particles of the material packed into a small space.

Compressibility (squashiness). Solids and liquids don't **compress** very much, so there can't be much space between the particles. Gases must have some space between particles, as they can be pushed together.

Stretching and flowing could be explained if there were particles held together by forces.

Diffusion could be explained if particles could move and spread out among themselves.

The particle theory

■ Observations on the properties of solids, liquids and gases led to the formation of the particle theory

Preliminary knowledge: The particle theory and states of matter

We can explain the three states of matter – solid, liquid and gas –
by the way the particles in the substances are arranged. (Remember
that the particles in the substance can be either atoms or molecules.)

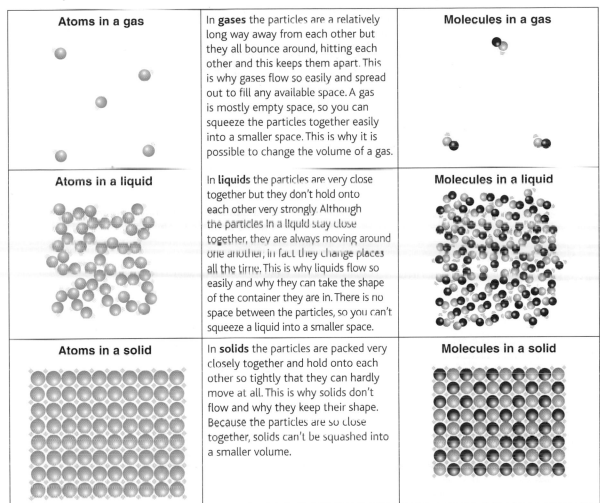

Atoms in a gas	In **gases** the particles are a relatively long way away from each other but they all bounce around, hitting each other and this keeps them apart. This is why gases flow so easily and spread out to fill any available space. A gas is mostly empty space, so you can squeeze the particles together easily into a smaller space. This is why it is possible to change the volume of a gas.	Molecules in a gas
Atoms in a liquid	In **liquids** the particles are very close together but they don't hold onto each other very strongly. Although the particles in a liquid stay close together, they are always moving around one another, in fact they change places all the time. This is why liquids flow so easily and why they can take the shape of the container they are in. There is no space between the particles, so you can't squeeze a liquid into a smaller space.	Molecules in a liquid
Atoms in a solid	In **solids** the particles are packed very closely together and hold onto each other so tightly that they can hardly move at all. This is why solids don't flow and why they keep their shape. Because the particles are so close together, solids can't be squashed into a smaller volume.	Molecules in a solid

Did you know?

Popping popcorn is all about liquids and vapours – actually water and steam (see the start of this chapter).

Each kernel (seed) of popcorn contains a tiny drop of water. The water is stored inside a sphere of soft starch and the soft starch is surrounded by a hard coat.

When you heat the kernels in a pan or microwave oven, the liquid water changes to vapour. This expands and puts pressure on the inside of the seed coat. When this pressure gets too much, the popcorn 'pops' and the steam escapes.

The hard bits left in the bottom of the popcorn are called 'old maids'. They are too dry to have a 'pop' in them!

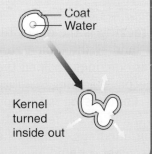

Coat
Water

Kernel turned inside out

◯ Particle theory and changes of state

When a substance changes state, from liquid to gas, for example, it does so because it absorbs energy. These changes of state can be explained by the particle theory.

Melting is when a solid is heated until it turns into a liquid. The energy from the heat (thermal energy) makes the particles in a solid vibrate more and more. Eventually they will have enough energy to break away from the other particles in the solid – the solid becomes a liquid.

Boiling is when a liquid is heated until it turns into a gas. The energy from the heat makes the particles in the liquid move around more quickly. Eventually they will have enough energy to escape from the liquid – the liquid becomes a gas.

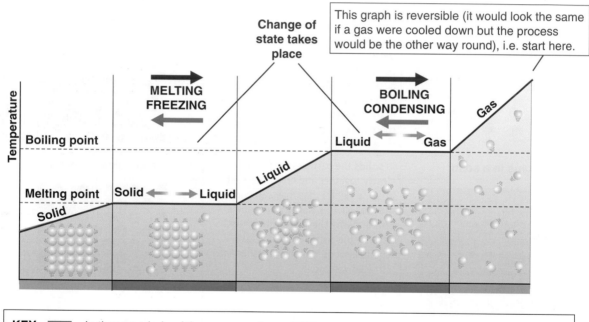

This graph is reversible (it would look the same if a gas were cooled down but the process would be the other way round), i.e. start here.

KEY

In these periods of time, **energy** is **used to push the particles apart** (so the 'line' graph stays flat).

In these periods of time, **energy** is **used to raise the temperature of the substance** (so the 'line' graph goes upwards).

Freezing is the opposite of melting. It is when a liquid becomes a solid as the temperature lowers. It loses energy as heat to its surroundings, making the particles move less and less – the liquid becomes a solid.

Condensing is the opposite of boiling. It is when a gas becomes a liquid as the temperature lowers. It loses energy as heat to its surroundings, making the particles move less and less – the gas becomes a liquid.

Sublimation is when a substance changes directly from a solid to a gas. **Deposition** is the opposite of sublimation – when a substance changes directly from a gas to a solid.

Heating and cooling of water

Water is a liquid at the sort of temperatures we find in a laboratory (that is, around 20 °C). When water is cooled, its temperature falls and the water eventually freezes. The liquid water changes state into solid water or **ice**. We can draw a graph of the temperature changes as water is cooled. This **cooling curve** for water is shown in the following diagram.

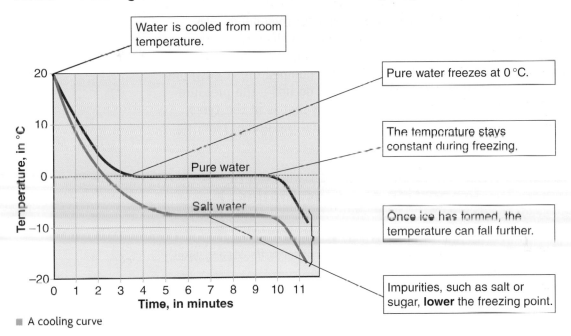

Water is cooled from room temperature.

Pure water freezes at 0 °C.

The temperature stays constant during freezing.

Pure water

Salt water

Once ice has formed, the temperature can fall further.

Impurities, such as salt or sugar, **lower** the freezing point.

■ A cooling curve

When water is heated, its temperature rises as the water molecules absorb thermal energy. Eventually the water boils and turns into water vapour (the gaseous state of water). The heating curve for water is shown in the following diagram.

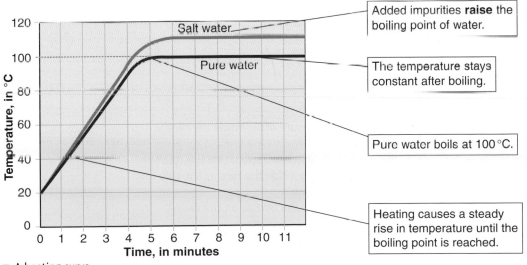

Added impurities **raise** the boiling point of water.

Salt water

Pure water

The temperature stays constant after boiling.

Pure water boils at 100 °C.

Heating causes a steady rise in temperature until the boiling point is reached.

■ A heating curve

In summary, therefore, water is a compound with a freezing point defined at 0 °C and a boiling point at 100 °C. There are two simple **chemical tests** for water. These have already been described at the start of this book in the Investigations in science section under the heading 'Useful chemical tests'.

Gas pressure

The particles in a gas move quickly and randomly; they bump into each other often. They also bump into the walls of their container. When they do this they cause pressure. This is called **gas pressure**.

Think about riding a bike. If your tyres are pumped up, it cushions you against the bumps in the road. Flat tyres do not – the pressure of the air inside them is too low. The more air that is in the tyres, the more particles hit the walls of the tyres and the higher the pressure.

Exercise 1.2: Properties of solids, liquids and gases

1 Copy and complete this table about the properties of solids, liquids and gases.

	Solids	Liquids	Gases
Do they flow easily?			
Can they be compressed?			
Can they change their shape?			
Are the particles close together or far apart?			
Do the particles hold onto each other tightly?			

2 Select a type of material for the following uses. Choose from solid, liquid or gas.
   (a) To act as a roof support.
   (b) To be squeezed into a container.
   (c) To be pushed through a pipe.
   (d) To fill up a balloon.
   (e) To make into a tool.
   (f) To pour from one container into another.

3 The tyre on a racing car is hard because of the pressure of air inside the tyre.
   (a) What causes the air pressure inside the tyre?
   (b) Why does the air pressure increase when the mechanics pump up the tyre?
   (c) Suggest what might happen to the air pressure inside the tyre as the tyre gets hotter during the race? Explain your answer.
   (d) How can tyres that contain air absorb some of the bumps on the racing circuit?

2 Elements and compounds

As we saw in Chapter 1, atoms are the simplest unit of matter. Molecules are made up of two or more atoms that are joined together. They can be atoms of the same type or groups of different atoms.

> Atoms are tiny! There are more than 5 million, million, million, million atoms in a glass of water.

Elements

A substance that is made of only one type of atom is called an **element**. For example, in the element aluminium there are only aluminium atoms. Aluminium, like every other element, cannot be broken down into simpler substances in the laboratory.

Each element is made up of many identical atoms.

There are more than 100 different kinds of atom, which means that there are more than 100 different elements. About 95 of these elements occur naturally on Earth. The other elements are made by nuclear reactions in special laboratories.

The English chemist John Dalton was the first scientist to state (in 1801) that all matter was composed of atoms. By the start of the twentieth century, however, other scientists had put forward a theory that atoms could be broken down further to even smaller particles, called **protons**, **electrons** and **neutrons**.

All of the atoms within an element behave in the same way, but they are different from the atoms in other elements. For example, atoms of gold are heavier than atoms of aluminium, so gold is a heavier metal than aluminium.

> **Did you know?**
>
> Each atom is made of even smaller particles. The number of some of these smaller particles, called **protons**, **electrons** and **neutrons**, is constant for each element. The number of protons in each atom is the **atomic number** for that element. For example, each **carbon atom** contains 6 protons and so the atomic number of carbon is 6.

Symbols and formulae for elements

Scientists have made up a series of symbols, called chemical symbols, for describing elements; this saves a lot of time when they need to write down the names of the elements many times! The symbol given to an element often comes from the first one or two letters of its name. The chemical symbol for oxygen is O, for example, and the chemical symbol for calcium is Ca. Some elements have chemical symbols that are not so obvious. The chemical symbol for iron is Fe. This is because iron was named when scientists still wrote down much of their work in Latin. The Latin name for iron is *ferrum*.

Some rules for chemical symbols:

- The first letter of a chemical symbol is *always* a capital letter. If there is a second letter it is always lower case.
- The chemical symbol is often the first one or two letters of the name of the element.
- Some elements get their chemical symbol from an old name, often from Latin.
- Every element has a different chemical symbol.

■ Some common elements with their chemical symbols

Aluminium	Al	Hydrogen	H	Oxygen	O
Calcium	Ca	Iron	Fe	Sodium	Na
Chlorine	Cl	Lead	Pb	Sulfur	S
Gold	Au	Nitrogen	N	Zinc	Zn
Carbon	C	Copper	Cu	Magnesium	Mg
Helium	He				

John Dalton

John Dalton (1766–1844) was an English chemist and physicist. He is best known for founding atomic theory, which states that all matter is composed of atoms are made up of smaller, subatomic particles – protons, electrons and neutrons.

He worked in Manchester, where a university laboratory and a city centre street are named after him. He was also colour-blind and was the first scientist to describe this condition and recognise that it is hereditary. Although his theories about what caused colour-blindness were later disproven, the condition is still sometimes to referred to as Daltonism.

In most elements the particles are individual atoms, but in a few elements the particles are molecules (that is, made up of two or more identical atoms bonded together). The **chemical formula** for an element tells us whether it is made of single atoms or of molecules. Some examples are shown in the following table.

■ Some elements with their chemical formulae

Name	Symbol of atoms	Diagram of particles	Formula of particles	Description of particles
Helium	He		He	Atoms
Magnesium	Mg		Mg	Atoms
Hydrogen	H		H_2	Molecules (each with two atoms)
Oxygen	O		O_2	Molecules (each with two atoms)
Sulfur	S		S_8	Molecules (each with eight atoms)

The Periodic Table

All the elements are listed in the **Periodic Table**. In this table:

- The elements are listed in order of their **atomic number** (the number of protons in the atom).
- The elements are shown as their **chemical symbols**.
- The elements are arranged in natural **groups** (particular types of metals, for example). Each group is a vertical column of elements that show similar properties.
- There is always a gradual change (called a 'trend') in the properties of the elements as you look across or down the table. Each vertical column showing a trend is called a **group** and each horizontal row showing a trend is called a **period**.

> The difference in properties between metals and non-metals is one of the most important pieces of information given by the Periodic Table.

Part of the Periodic Table is shown in the following diagram.

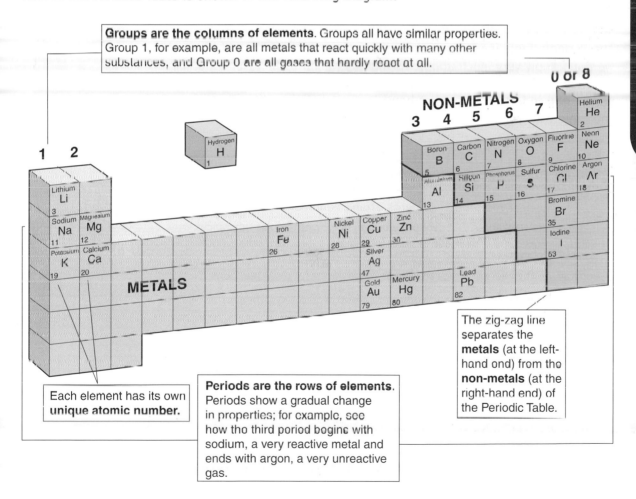

Groups are the columns of elements. Groups all have similar properties. Group 1, for example, are all metals that react quickly with many other substances, and Group 0 are all gases that hardly react at all.

Each element has its own **unique atomic number.**

Periods are the rows of elements. Periods show a gradual change in properties; for example, see how the third period begins with sodium, a very reactive metal and ends with argon, a very unreactive gas.

The zig-zag line separates the **metals** (at the left-hand end) from the **non-metals** (at the right-hand end) of the Periodic Table.

Dimitri Mendeléev

The arrangement of elements as shown by the Periodic Table was worked out by a Russian scientist called Mendeléev in 1869.

Dimitri Ivanovich Mendeléev was born in 1834 in Siberia, the youngest of 15 children. His father went blind when Dimitri was young and his mother struggled to bring up the family while running a glass factory. She saved to send Dimitri to be educated, though she died exhausted shortly after he started his studies at St Petersburg.

In addition to his research work, Dimitri was a brilliant chemistry teacher. Everyone wanted to come to his lectures. At that time women were not allowed in university classes, so Dimitri gave extra classes for women in his spare time.

Dimitri was a very down-to-earth person and was happy to travel third class in trains along with the peasants. He only cut his hair once a year, in spring when the warm weather started!

Using the Periodic Table

The Periodic Table is very useful for predicting the properties of elements we don't know very much about. As long as we know the atomic number of an element, we will have some idea of its properties. The table is also very useful in letting us predict how elements listed in different parts of the table will react together.

Exercise 2.1: The Periodic Table

1 Copy and complete the following sentences using words from this list:

nuclear, molecules, elements, atoms, hundred

_____ are substances that cannot be broken down into simpler substances. Some, such as carbon, are made of particles called _____ and others, such as oxygen, are made of particles called _____. There are about a _____ of these substances. The heaviest ones can only be made during _____ reactions.

2 Which of these substances are elements: carbon, water, sugar, magnesium, sulfur, air, lead?

◯ Metals and non-metals

There are two basic types of element: **metals** and **non-metals**. Of the elements that occur naturally, about three-quarters are metals and one-quarter are non-metals. The metals are arranged on the left-hand side of the Periodic Table with the non-metals on the right.

Look back at the diagram of the Periodic Table. You can see that the metals and non-metals are separated by a zig-zag line. The metals close to the line have some of the properties of non-metals and the non-metals close to the line have some of the properties of metals. The important physical properties of metals are shown on the next page and the properties of metals and non-metals are compared in the table that follows.

Metals

The properties of metals can be explained by particle theory.

Some metals are **tough**; they don't break easily because there are very strong bonds between the particles.

Some metals are **shiny**; they reflect light, especially when they are polished or cut.

Metals **conduct electricity**. This happens because metal particles can pass on the electrical charge from one to another.

Metals can be **stretched or hammered into different shapes**. The bonds between the particles are strong enough to stop the metal from breaking, even when the particles are rearranged.

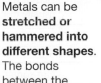

Most metals have **high melting points (mp) and boiling points (bp)**. This means they can absorb a great deal of energy before they melt. This is because the metal particles (atoms) are joined to each other by strong bonds. (Sodium and mercury are exceptions with low mps.)

Metals **conduct thermal (internal) energy**. The hot particles vibrate strongly. They move and pass energy from particle to particle.

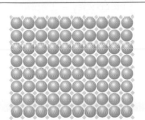

Most metals have **high densities**, which means they feel heavier for their size because they have many particles packed closely together into a small volume. (Sodium and potassium are exceptions; they float on water.)

Some metals are **magnetic**, which means they can be attracted by magnets. (You will learn a lot more about magnetism in Physics.) Only iron, nickel or cobalt (or alloys made from these metals) are magnetic.

Metals can make **alloys**. An alloy is a combination of different metals, which has combined properties of the different metals. For example, an alloy wheel combines lightness from one metal with strength from another.

METALS	NON-METALS
Found on the **left**-hand side of the Periodic Table	Found on the **right**-hand side of the Periodic Table
Usually **solids** at room temperature	Usually **solids** or **gases** at room temperature
Good **conductors of electricity**	Poor conductors of electricity, therefore good **insulators**
Good **conductors of thermal (internal) energy**	Poor conductors of thermal (internal) energy, therefore good **insulators**
Shiny (**lustrous**) when they are polished or cut	Do not reflect light very well and so are usually **dull**
Malleable (can be hammered into a different shape)	Most are **brittle** (they break if they are hammered)
Sonorous (sound like a bell when they are hit)	Not sonorous
Ductile (can be stretched)	Not ductile
Usually very **dense**	Have a **low density**
Have **high melting and boiling points**	Usually have **low melting and boiling points**
Strong and tough, so they are very **hard-wearing**	Not strong or tough, so not hard-wearing

Did you know?

Mercury is the only metal that is a liquid at room temperature. Mercury used to be used in thermometers but it is now largely being replaced with non-toxic alternatives.

What properties do you think mercury has that makes it useful in thermometers?

There are also some important differences in the chemical properties of metals and non-metals. These will be looked at when we study some of the chemical reactions of metals and non-metals in Chapters 7 and 8.

Non-metals

The simplest way to tell a metal from a non-metal is that most non-metals do not conduct thermal energy or electricity. The following diagram shows a simple circuit that can be used for testing the electrical conductivity of a material.

There is one non-metal that is a good conductor of electricity – graphite, a form of carbon.

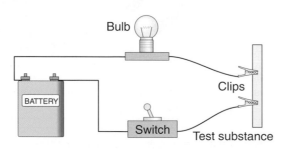

Many non-metals are very good **thermal insulators** (they do not conduct thermal energy very well). Gases are especially poor conductors of thermal energy because the molecules of a gas are too far apart to pass thermal energy from one to another.

It is very important to look at more than one property if you are trying to decide whether a material is a metal or non-metal. For example, most metals are solids but mercury is a liquid at room temperature and most solid non-metals are very brittle, although the hardest natural substance is diamond (a form of carbon, which is a non-metal).

The photographs that follow show how different non-metals can be from one another. At room temperature some are solids, some are gases and there is one that is a liquid!

■ Sulfur powder

■ Carbon (diamond)

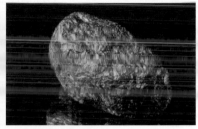

■ Carbon (graphite)

■ Bromine liquid and vapour in a jar

■ Chlorine gas in a jar

■ Phosphorus under water in a jar

Non-metals form much of our world

Although there are not as many non-metals as metals, most of the objects around us are made from non-metals. See the diagram on the next page.

Many **man-made (synthetic) substances** contain large amounts of non-metals. For example, plastics are mostly made up of carbon and hydrogen.

Dry **air** is a mixture of non-metals. These are all gases.

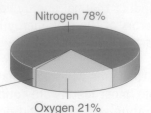

Nitrogen 78%

Other elements, including carbon (carbon dioxide) and inert gases, 1%

Oxygen 21%

The **sea** is a mixture of substances. Because the sea is mainly water, most of it is made up of the elements hydrogen and oxygen. There are still quantities of metals dissolved in seawater.

Oxygen 91%

Other elements including silicon, aluminium, gold, calcium, iodine, potassium, bromine 0.4%

Sodium 1.0%
Chlorine 1.9%
Hydrogen 5.7%

The **body** is mainly made up of non-metals. Most of the metal is calcium in teeth and bones, sodium in blood plasma and iron in red blood cells.

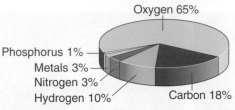

Oxygen 65%

Phosphorus 1%
Metals 3%
Nitrogen 3%
Hydrogen 10%
Carbon 18%

Exercise 2.2: Metals and non-metals

1 Copy and complete the following sentences:
   (a) _____ form much of our world.
   (b) Air is mostly a mixture of nitrogen and _____. Other elements, such as _____ and _____, are found in much smaller proportions.
   (c) The most common element in the sea is _____, followed by _____.
   (d) Most metals are solids. The exception is _____, which is liquid at room temperature. Metals are usually much tougher than non-metals, although the non-metal _____ is the hardest natural material on the Earth.
   (e) The most common difference between metals and non-metals is that metals are good _____ of thermal energy and electricity, whereas non-metals tend to be _____.

2 This table shows the percentage, by weight, of different elements in the Earth's crust.

Aluminium	8.0
Calcium	3.5
Magnesium	2.0
Iron	5.0
Oxygen	46.5
Potassium	2.5
Sodium	3.0
Silicon	27.5
Other elements	2.0

Working Scientifically

   (a) Plot a pie chart of these percentages.
   (b) Which is the most abundant metal on Earth?
   (c) Find out where would you find most of the silicon on the Earth.
   (d) If you had a sample of these pure elements, how could you separate the iron from the other elements?
   (e) Find out which non-metal is not shown here but is a large part of the human body.

⬡ Compounds

As we have seen, elements are made of only one type of atom and each element has its own particular properties. Metallic and non-metallic elements have very different properties.

Elements can combine during chemical reactions to form new substances. When two or more different elements combine they form a **compound**. Compounds can have very different properties to the elements from which they are formed, as we will see in the next section.

The particles in a compound are called **molecules**. These molecules are all the same in one particular compound but they contain atoms of more than one element.

When atoms of elements combine during a chemical reaction (see Chapter 7), the link between them is called a **chemical bond**.

Here are **atoms** of carbon and oxygen. They are two different elements. These are the **reactants** in this chemical reaction.	These atoms can combine to form a **molecule** of carbon dioxide. The atoms of carbon and oxygen are linked by **chemical bonds**. Carbon dioxide is the **product** of this chemical reaction.

◼ Different elements can combine to produce a new compound

Go further

Chemical bonds

The formation of chemical bonds depends on the electrons in the atoms.

- Sometimes electrons are *shared* between atoms, making **covalent bonds**.
- Sometimes electrons *pass from* one atom to another, making **ionic bonds**.

Elements and compounds have different properties

Hydrogen and oxygen are elements. Hydrogen is a colourless gas that is flammable (will burn) and oxygen is a colourless gas that helps other substances to burn. If these two substances are mixed and then the mixture is heated, a **chemical reaction** takes place. This reaction produces a new substance, water, and this new substance has very different properties from the two elements that made it. Water is a colourless liquid that puts fires out! This new substance is a compound. See the diagram on the next page.

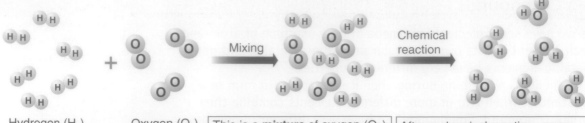

Hydrogen (H$_2$)   Oxygen (O$_2$)   Mixing   Chemical reaction

| This is a **mixture** of oxygen (O$_2$) and hydrogen (H$_2$). This mixture would have the **same** properties as the two elements. | After a chemical reaction, a new compound, water (H$_2$O), has been formed. This compound has totally different properties from the two elements which reacted together. |

We can write a shorter version of what has happened in this reaction in the form of a **chemical word equation** (see Chapter 7). The word equation for the reaction between oxygen and hydrogen is:

hydrogen + oxygen → water

Another important example that shows the main features of a chemical reaction is the reaction between the two elements iron and sulfur.

> You may sometimes see 'sulfur' spelled 'sulphur', especially in older books. Both mean the same thing but you should be aware that 'sulfur' with an 'f' is now the accepted standard spelling.

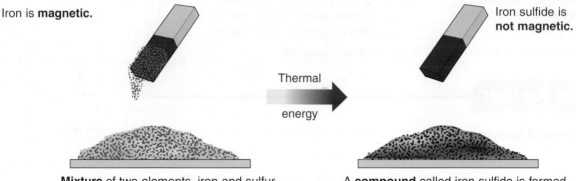

Iron is **magnetic.**

Thermal energy

Iron sulfide is **not magnetic.**

Mixture of two elements, iron and sulfur   A **compound** called iron sulfide is formed.

iron + sulfur → iron sulfide
(thermal energy)

Working Scientifically

Investigation: How do compounds differ from elements?

The aim of this experiment is to investigate some of the ways in which compounds differ from elements.

Your teacher will demonstrate the formation of iron sulfide.

Carry out the following tests and record your results in a table like the one on the next page.

Substance	Appearance	Action of a magnet	Behaviour when added to water
The element sulfur (S)			
The element iron (Fe)			
Mixture of iron and sulfur			
The compound iron sulfide			

1 Describe the differences between the mixture of iron and sulfur and the compound iron sulfide.
2 Name the property of iron that allows it to be separated from a mixture of iron and sulfur. Does iron sulfide have this same property?
3 Name two other compounds that contain sulfur, and one that contains iron. These should be compounds that you have studied.

The fixed number of atoms in a compound is very different from a mixture. In a mixture there could be any number of atoms. For example, CO_2 is a **compound**, but a **mixture** of carbon and oxygen could have 1000 times as much carbon as oxygen, or only one-tenth as much!

The formulae of compounds

When elements combine to form a compound there is always a fixed number of atoms. This allows us to write a **chemical formula** for the compound. A chemical formula is a way of showing a compound as a set of symbols.

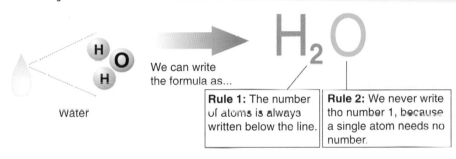

water

We can write the formula as...

H_2O

Rule 1: The number of atoms is always written below the line.

Rule 2: We never write the number 1, because a single atom needs no number.

It is **very important** to remember that a formula like CO means that the compound contains carbon (symbol C) and oxygen (symbol O). If you mixed up capital and small letters, you might write Co, which is the symbol for the element cobalt. **So be very careful not to mix up capital and small letters!**

Names for different compounds

The naming of compounds is based on some general rules, though there are some exceptions. If you learn the following simple rules, you will be able to work out the name of most compounds easily.

- If **only two elements** are combined, then the name of the compound ends in **-ide**. If one of the elements is a metal, then the name of the metal comes first. For example:
  Sodium chlor**ide** (NaCl) is made from sodium and chlorine.
  Magnesium ox**ide** (MgO) is made from magnesium and oxygen.
- If the compound contains **more than one atom of one of its elements** then you might use **mono-, di-** or **tri-** in its name. This can be very useful in telling some similar compounds apart. For example:
  Carbon **mono**xide (CO) has only one oxygen atom, whereas carbon **di**oxide (CO_2) has two oxygen atoms.

Compounds called 'alkanes' are an exception. They only consist of hydrogen and carbon atoms. The first part of their name is determined by the number of carbons and the second part is 'ane'. For example, CH_4 is called methane.

- When **three or more different elements** combine, and the third one is oxygen, the name will end in **-ate**.
  For example:
  Potassium sulf**ate** (K_2SO_4) contains potassium, sulfur and oxygen.
  Sodium nitr**ate** ($NaNO_3$) contains sodium, nitrogen and oxygen.
  Calcium carbon**ate** ($CaCO_3$) contains calcium, carbon and oxygen.

  Note: Compounds called 'hydroxides' are an exception. They contain a metal, oxygen and hydrogen but the oxygen and hydrogen are both included in the name of the compound. For example, NaOH is sodium hydroxide, **not** sodium hydrate.

Here are the names and chemical formulae for some compounds that you should learn and remember:

Compound	Chemical formula	Compound	Chemical formula
Water	H_2O	Hydrogen chloride	HCl
Carbon monoxide	CO	Sodium hydroxide	NaOH
Carbon dioxide	CO_2	Calcium carbonate	$CaCO_3$
Methane	CH_4	Copper sulfate	$CuSO_4$
Sodium chloride	NaCl	Sulfuric acid	H_2SO_4

Some compounds have 'common' names. For example sodium chloride (NaCl) is common salt.

Exercise 2.3: Compounds

1 Copy and complete this table to compare the properties of elements and compounds:

Name of substance	Chemical symbol or formula	Solid, liquid or gas	Colour	Does it conduct electricity?	Any special property?
Iron					
Sulfur					
Iron sulfide					
Oxygen					
Hydrogen					
Water					

2 (a) What is a compound?
  (b) Which of the following substances are compounds?
      Al_2O_3, NaCl, He, HCl, CO, Cl_2, K, H_2O, Na, Co

3 Which elements are found in the following compounds?
 (a) sodium nitrate (b) magnesium carbonate
 (c) calcium carbide (d) nitrogen hydroxide
 (e) aluminium oxide (f) hydrogen sulfate

4 Look at the diagrams in the following table.

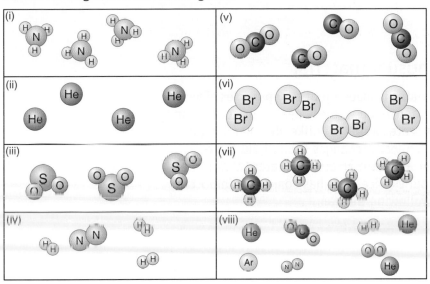

Which of these are:
 (a) elements (b) compounds
 (c) mixtures (d) made up only of atoms
 (e) made up only of molecules?

Extension question

5 Look at this simplified Periodic Table and then answer the questions that follow.

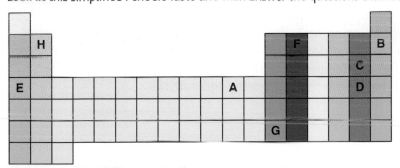

 (a) Which two elements would you expect to have very similar properties?
 (b) Which element is a very unreactive gas?
 (c) Which element is likely to have some properties of a metal and some properties of a non-metal?

③ Water

Water is an unusual material

Like all other materials, water is made up of tiny particles. These particles can change position when water is heated or cooled, and so the water can change its state. Water is unlike all other substances, however, because when it freezes (changes from liquid to solid), it **expands**. This means that a certain amount of water takes up less space than the same amount of ice. This has some very important results, as shown in the following diagram.

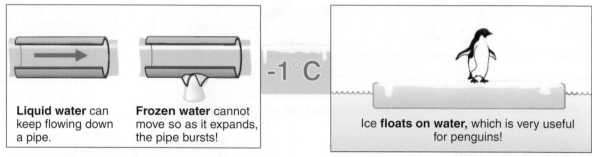

Liquid water can keep flowing down a pipe.

Frozen water cannot move so as it expands, the pipe bursts!

-1°C

Ice **floats on water,** which is very useful for penguins!

■ Freezing of water – the good news and the bad news

We know that ice melts and water boils at definite, specific temperatures (the melting and boiling points). Water can also change state from liquid to vapour (a gas) more slowly and this change of state (**evaporation**) can occur at any temperature. The rate at which evaporation occurs depends on how much thermal energy the particles have; they may have enough of this energy to escape their attraction to other water particles and become water vapour.

> You will learn about evaporation as a technique used for separating some mixtures in Chapter 5, 'Separating solids and water'.

The water cycle

Scientists think that the amount of water on the Earth has stayed the same for millions of years. However, the water is constantly recycling as it changes from one state to another. Water **evaporates** from the sea into the air and then **condenses** back from the air into the sea. In between evaporation and condensation, water may be moved over thousands of kilometres by winds. These natural changes in the state of water are called the **water cycle** and are illustrated in the following diagram.

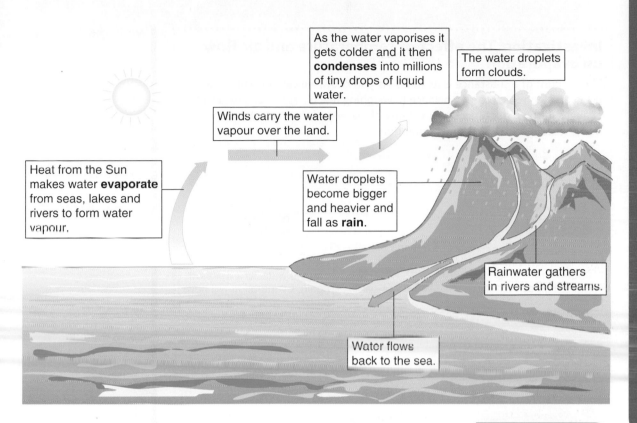

As the water vaporises it gets colder and it then **condenses** into millions of tiny drops of liquid water.

The water droplets form clouds.

Winds carry the water vapour over the land.

Heat from the Sun makes water **evaporate** from seas, lakes and rivers to form water vapour.

Water droplets become bigger and heavier and fall as **rain**.

Rainwater gathers in rivers and streams.

Water flows back to the sea.

The heating of water to evaporate it from the sea is caused by the Sun. Remembering how the Sun also supplied the energy for plants to make their food, and that water is one of the raw materials for this process (look at photosynthesis in Biology, Chapter 8) you can see why the Sun and water are absolutely essential for all life on Earth.

Winds and solar energy affect the water cycle. An increase in temperature makes water evaporate more quickly from the sea and from rivers and lakes, and winds move the water vapour in the air from place to place.

Scientists are very concerned about the effects of global warming caused by the production of greenhouse gases (see Chapter 7) and are trying to predict how rising temperatures will affect our climate and our lives. So that they can predict what will happen in nature, scientists carry out experiments in the laboratory and use the results to explain what might happen in the outside environment. Carrying out an experiment and using the results to make predictions like this is called making a **model**.

After carrying out many experiments of the type given in the Investigation below, experts in the study of weather have **predicted** that global warming will make the seas evaporate more quickly. As a result, there will be many more violent rainstorms and strong winds (more hurricanes) as all this extra water is carried over the land.

Did you know?
All water has been recycled. The water you drink could have been drunk by someone else, thousands of years ago!

Working Scientifically

Investigation: The effect of temperature and air flow on evaporation

The amount of a substance is its **mass**. As you know, we can measure mass using an electronic top-pan balance (a weighing machine). We can measure changes in the mass of a certain volume of water and then calculate how much water has been lost by evaporation.

A beaker containing 100 cm³ of water is weighed on an electronic balance.

LEAVE FOR 5 DAYS

Five days later the beaker and the water are weighed again. Evaporation will have caused some of the mass of water to be lost.

■ Measuring the evaporation of water

The experiment can be repeated at **different temperatures** to make a model of the effect of temperature on loss of water by evaporation.

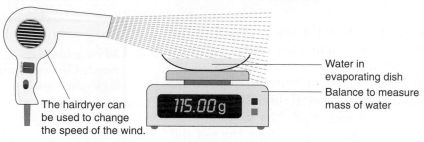

The hairdryer can be used to change the speed of the wind.

Water in evaporating dish

Balance to measure mass of water

■ Measuring the effect of airflow on evaporation

The experiment can also be repeated with **different speeds of air flow** to make a model of the effect of windspeed on the loss of water by evaporation. Use a hairdryer on its cool setting, changing the speed setting.

A stopclock is used to measure the time that the wind is blowing over the water. You can then calculate the **rate** of water loss.

$$\text{rate of water loss} = \frac{\text{change in mass}}{\text{time}}$$

1 Give **two** reasons why hanging out washing helps the washing to dry.

Extension question

2 Hurricanes are more common in tropical areas of the world. Find out why.

Exercise 3.1: Water and the water cycle

1 Copy and complete this paragraph:

Pure water boils at _____ and freezes at _____. A simple chemical test uses
cobalt chloride paper to test for the presence of water. The cobalt chloride paper
changes from _____ to _____ if water is present. Seawater is a _____ of many
different substances. The presence of impurities in seawater _____ the freezing
point and _____ the boiling point of water.

2 Look at the investigation below into the effect of temperature on evaporation.

Working Scientifically

Investigation: Does warm air speed up evaporation?

A clock or stopwatch
can measure
the time taken for the
cloth to dry out.

An electric hairdryer
has three settings:
cool, warm and hot.

A cloth can be soaked
in water.

We will change one factor: the thermal energy from the dryer. We will then
measure one other factor: the time taken for the cloth to dry out.

To make it a fair test, we must keep the other factors the same:

- the speed the fan is blowing
- the distance between the dryer and the cloth
- the size of the cloth
- the fabric of the cloth
- the amount of water added to the dry cloth.

How could you change the experiment to test:

(a) whether the speed of blowing the air affected the rate of evaporation
(b) whether different types of cloth dry off at different rates.

Write your answers in a table like this:

Experiment	Factor to change (independent variable)	Factor to measure (dependent variable)	Factors to keep constant (control variables)
(a)			
(b)			

4 Pure substance or mixture?

Chemistry is the study of the properties and reactions of substances. A chemist is interested in how different substances are made up and how they can be changed.

It is very important in chemistry to know whether a substance is **pure**, or whether it is made of several different substances mixed together. A doctor, for example, would want to be absolutely sure that a drug was pure before it was offered to a patient. A pure substance may behave in a different way from a **mixture**.

Remember:

- In a pure substance **all the particles are the same** and so they all behave in the same way.
- In a mixture there is **more than one type of particle**. The particles are not joined together and the mixture can react in different ways, depending on how many of each type of particle is present.

> Making a mixture is an example of a physical change not a chemical change. You will learn more about these two types of changes to materials in Chapter 6.

Pure ethanol contains only ethanol particles and all of them are very poisonous.

Drinks like lager and beer contain a mixture of different particles: alcohol, minerals, sugars, carbon dioxide and about 95% water.

Preliminary knowledge: Testing for purity

There are a number of different methods that can be used to test whether a substance is pure or is a mixture.

- **Appearance**: sometimes the particles are big enough to be seen, perhaps with a microscope. For example, if you study a sample of soil, you will see that it is made up of several different types of particle, so it is a mixture.
- **Melting and boiling point measurements**: a pure substance always melts at one fixed temperature and boils at another fixed temperature (see Chapter 1). A mixture can have very different melting and boiling points, depending on how much of each substance is present.
- **Looking for particular physical properties**: some metals are magnetic, for example, and can be separated from mixtures using a magnet.

Soil sample

Look at the soil sample in the diagram. The particles are large enough to see that it is a mixture. Different types of soil have different properties, depending on how many of each type of particle are present.

Pure water

The liquid in the diagram is pure water. We know that because it boils at 100 °C. A mixture, for example salt solution, has different boiling and melting points, depending on the amount of each substance dissolved in it.

Mixture of iron filings and copper

This diagram shows a mixture of iron filings and copper. We can tell that this is a mixture because the iron is attracted to the magnet but the copper is left behind. Some mixtures can be separated easily like this. For more information on the separation of mixtures, see Chapter 5.

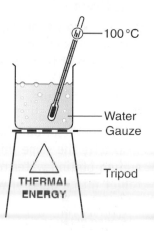

■ There are different types of particle in this soil sample

■ Pure water boils at 100 °C

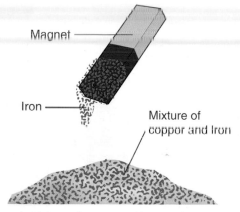

■ A mixture of copper and iron can be separated with a magnet

Exercise 4.1: Pure substance or mixture?

1 Give two ways that you could check that a mixture of sand and salt actually contained two different types of particle.
2 A delicatessen sells bottles of 'pure mountain spring water'. How could you check whether this claim is true?
3 A popular brand of orange juice claims to be 'pure orange juice, containing only natural fruit sugar, vitamin C, citric acid and water'. What is wrong with this claim?
4 How could you tell whether a metallic powder contained only iron filings or whether it also had some magnesium mixed in with it?

Working Scientifically

More about mixtures: solutions and solubility

As you have seen, a pure substance is made up of only one type of particle. A mixture is made up of different types of particle.

Making a mixture is an example of a physical change; it is **not** a chemical change (see Chapter 6).

Preliminary knowledge: Solids can dissolve to make solutions

You will know that the appearance of some substances changes when they are mixed with water. You can see this if you drop a sugar cube into a cup of tea; the sugar seems to disappear. In fact what has happened is that the solid sugar cube has **dissolved** in the liquid to form a mixture. This mixture is a **solution** and the sugar has not disappeared at all. The particles of the sugar have spread so that you can't see them, but they are still there.

Exactly the same thing happens when you make a cup of coffee by adding boiling water to coffee granules or when you put an aspirin tablet into a glass of water.

> One 5 g sugar cube dissolved in 200 g of tea will give 205 g of sugary-tea solution. This supports the principle of the conservation of mass, which you will learn about in Chapter 6.

Coffee granules dissolve in hot water to produce a solution of coffee.

Sugar dissolves in coffee to make a sweet sugary solution.

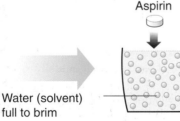
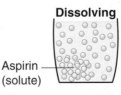

> **Did you know?**
> It is not just solids that can dissolve in water. Gaseous oxygen can dissolve in water enabling fish to breathe. Some liquids, including alcohol, can also dissolve.

Aspirin

Water (solvent) full to brim

Aspirin (solute)

Dissolving

Dissolved

The solvent particles have space between them and can move about.

The solute particles dissolve ...

... and spread out between the solvent particles.

An aspirin dissolves in water to make a solution.

What makes up a solution?

If a substance will dissolve to form a solution, we say that the substance is **soluble**. The substance that dissolves is called the **solute** and the substance it dissolves in is called the **solvent**.

In other words:

solution = solute + solvent

When a solution is formed, a chemical change is **not** involved. A solution is a mixture in which the solute and solvent particles are arranged randomly, but that may be separated using physical techniques. You will find out how to separate the different substances in a solution in the next chapter.

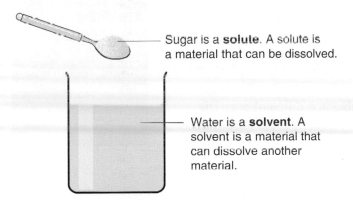

Sugar is a **solute**. A solute is a material that can be dissolved.

Water is a **solvent**. A solvent is a material that can dissolve another material.

The sugar has not disappeared. The water particles spread the sugar particles out so much that we can no longer see them.

If the mixture is clear, even if it is coloured like black coffee, it is a solution.

■ The sugar has dissolved in the water to make a solution

Working Scientifically

Investigation: Boiling points

The aim of this experiment is to find the boiling point of water and two different sodium chloride (common salt) solutions.

The concentration of these sodium chloride solutions can be expressed as a percentage. For example, a 1 per cent solution contains 1g of sodium chloride (the solute) dissolved in 100g of water (the solvent).

Your teacher will demonstrate experiments to find the boiling points of water and two different common salt solutions. Record the boiling points in the table below.

	Water	Dilute (2%) common salt solution	Concentrated (10%) common salt solution
Boiling point			

1 What temperature does **pure** water always boil at?
2 What do you notice about the boiling points of the common salt solutions (mixtures)?

Insoluble solids form suspensions

If a substance will not dissolve in a solvent, we say that the substance is **insoluble**.

A good example of an insoluble substance is chalk in water. Chalk will not dissolve in water, so when the two substances are mixed, the mixture stays cloudy because the chalk particles stay stuck together in pieces that are big enough for us to see. This kind of mixture is called a **suspension**.

You can see a good example of a suspension when carbon dioxide is bubbled through limewater; the cloudy liquid is actually a suspension of chalk (calcium carbonate, to give chalk its chemical name).

Some insoluble material settles to the bottom of a container of solvent; this is called the **sediment**.

Another good example of a suspension is a mixture of sand and water; sandy water is very cloudy indeed!

Water as a solvent

Water is a very common solvent, but it is not the only one. A substance that is insoluble in one solvent can be soluble in a different one. The **solubility** of a substance is a measure of the amount of a substance that will dissolve in a particular solvent at a given temperature. Many industries depend on substances having a different solubility in different solvents.

So, it is important to remember that water is not the only solvent and not all solutes are soluble in water. For example, some stains on clothing cannot be removed by water, especially greasy or oily stains, but other solvents (like those used by dry cleaners) can dissolve and remove these difficult stains.

The following table details some other common solvents and how they are used.

■ A mixture of chalk and water form a suspension (middle). If left for a period of time the chalk settles to the bottom of the water, forming sediment (bottom).

■ Some common solvents in everyday use

Substance (solute)	Solvent	Important point
Pigment in gloss paint	White spirit	Paint colour does not dissolve when it rains.
Pleasant smelling oils in perfume and aftershave	Alcohol (ethanol)	Alcohol evaporates after spraying, leaving a pleasant smell behind.
Pigment in nail varnish	Propanone	Nail varnish doesn't wash off easily.
Correcting fluid (Tipp-Ex) contains a white pigment in a fatty solvent	Fatty solvent	Solvent evaporates and leaves white pigment particles behind.

It is important to understand that certain solvents can be very **harmful**. Some solvents can dissolve away fats in the cell membranes. Cells can burst and injury or death can result. Do **not** sniff solvents!

Temperature and solubility

You can tell if a substance has dissolved in water because the substance seems to disappear and the solution is clear. However, you can't just keep on dissolving a substance; eventually no more will dissolve and some of the substance will begin to settle at the bottom of the container.

When this happens, we say that the solution is saturated. No more particles of the solute can be fitted between the particles of the solvent and so the undissolved particles of the solute stick together. The amount of solute that will dissolve in a solvent, or the rate of dissolving, is referred to as its solubility.

Scientists can use the settling of a substance at saturation to investigate how different conditions affect the solubility of substances.

Preliminary knowledge: Factors affecting the rate of dissolving

Some important factors that affect the **rate** at which a substance will dissolve are:

- the amount of **mixing** or **stirring** that goes on
- the **temperature** of the solvent
- the **size of the solute particles** (whether the solute is in lumps or has been ground down to a powder).

The way temperature affects solubility can be investigated by measuring the amount of solute that will dissolve in 100 g of water at different temperatures. The results of an example of this type of investigation are shown on the graph below.

Working Scientifically

The amount of **solute** that dissolves depends on how much **solvent** is present. The figure for **solubility** is always given as 'grams of solute per 100 g of water'.

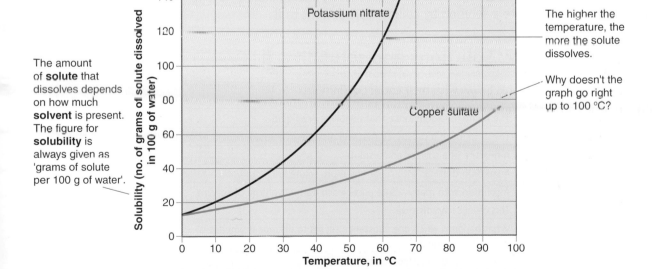

The higher the temperature, the more the solute dissolves.

Why doesn't the graph go right up to 100 °C?

Investigation: Limits to solubility

The aim of this experiment is to investigate whether there are limits to the amount of solute that will dissolve in a solvent.

You will be given one of three solids: sodium chloride (common salt), sodium hydrogen carbonate (bicarbonate of soda) and potassium nitrate.

Prediction: Do you think that there is a limit to the amount of solute that will dissolve in a solvent, or can you go on adding more forever? Explain your answer.

You will carry out an experiment to test your prediction. What things will you have to keep the same to make sure that this is a fair test? These are your control variables.

Discuss your ideas with your teacher and then try out your experiment. When you have completed this, your teacher may ask you to investigate the solubility of the other substances and compare the results.

Safety: Potassium nitrate is an oxidising agent and so can be dangerous. Follow the safety instructions given by your teacher.

1 What is a saturated solution?
2 What is solubility?
3 Name two factors that affect solubility.

Dilute or concentrated?

A solution with many solute particles in a certain volume of solvent is said to be **concentrated** (this is a scientific way of saying that it is strong). A solution with very few solute particles in the same volume of solvent is **dilute** (or weak). We can concentrate a solution by adding more solute to it and we can dilute a solution by adding more solvent to it.

Exercise 4.2: Solutions and solubility

1 Match up the words below with their correct definitions.

Dissolve	The name for a substance that dissolves in a liquid
Concentrated	The amount of a substance that will dissolve in a liquid
Dilute	A mixture of a solvent and a solute
Solute	A solution that cannot accept any more solute
Soluble	A solution with many solute particles in a small volume of solvent
Solvent	This means 'can dissolve'
Solution	What happens when one substance seems to disappear when it is mixed with a liquid
Insoluble	A solution with very few solute particles
Saturated	The name for the liquid part of a solution
Solubility	This means 'cannot dissolve'

2 Cola is a solution.

(a) Use books or the internet to find out three main solutes and the solvent in cola.

(b) Cola manufacturers want the manufacturing process to take as little time as possible. How can they make sure that the solutes dissolve quickly in the solvent?

3 The following diagram shows an experiment to dissolve a solute.

Working Scientifically

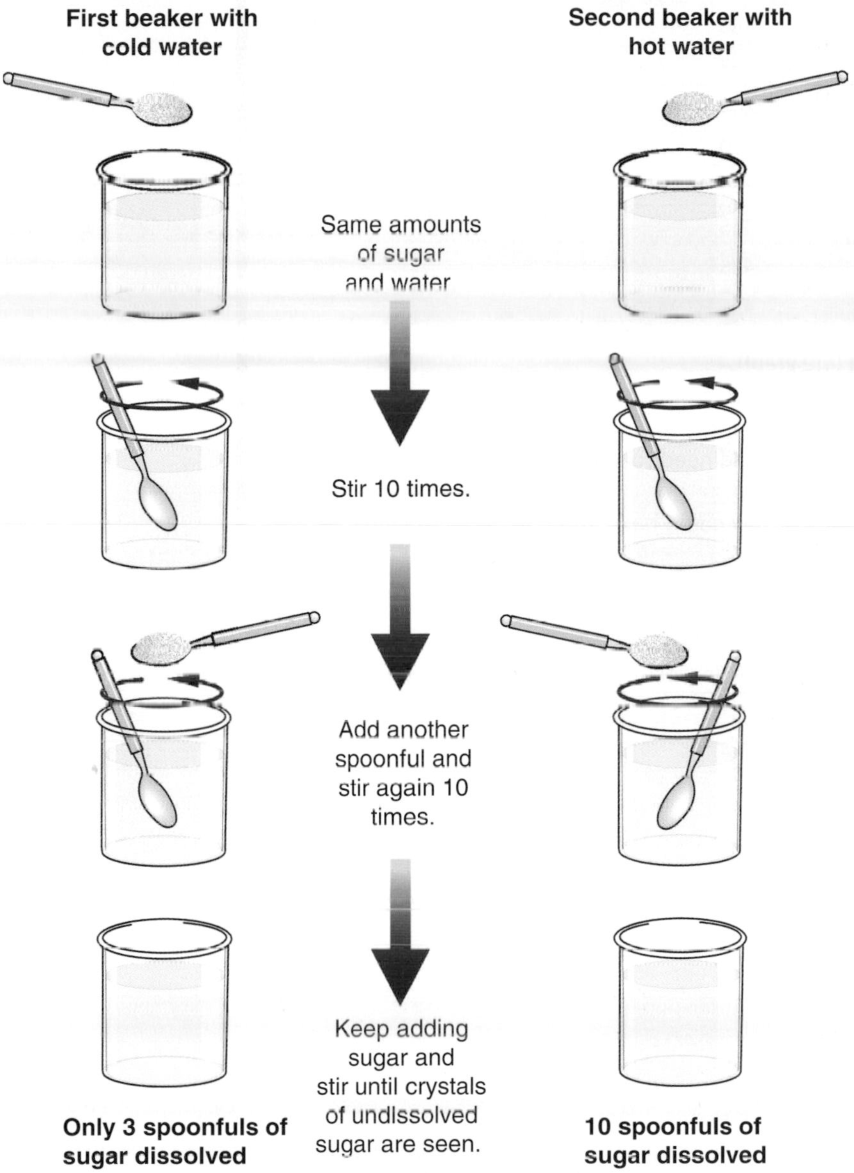
First beaker with cold water
Second beaker with hot water
Same amounts of sugar and water
Stir 10 times.
Add another spoonful and stir again 10 times.
Keep adding sugar and stir until crystals of undissolved sugar are seen.
Only 3 spoonfuls of sugar dissolved
10 spoonfuls of sugar dissolved

(a) What is the independent (input) variable in this experiment?

(b) What is the dependent (outcome) variable in this experiment?

(c) What has the scientist done to make sure that this is a fair test?

(d) How could you alter the experiment to investigate the effect of lump size on the solubility of sugar?

Extension question

4 Amna and her friend Izzy decided to investigate the solubility of sugar in water. They added weighed amounts of sugar to a beaker containing 100 g of water until no more sugar could dissolve. They repeated the experiment but varied the water temperature. Here are their results:

Temperature/°C	Mass of sugar that dissolves in 100 g of water/grams
0	180
10	192
20	205
30	220
50	265
70	365
80	425
90	475

(a) Plot their results as a line graph.

(b) How much sugar dissolves in 100 g of water at 40 °C?

(c) How much sugar would dissolve in 250 g of water at 50 °C?

(d) Give two factors that they would need to keep constant if this were to be a fair test.

(e) Suggest two ways in which they could have improved the reliability of their results.

5 Separating mixtures of materials

As you have seen, a **pure** substance is one in which all of the particles (atoms or molecules) are the same. A **mixture** contains different types of particle. Remember that different materials have **different useful properties**.

Air, tap water and seawater are good examples of mixtures. They are made up of different particles that are not combined with one another. Because they are **not joined by chemical bonds**, these particles can be separated using **physical methods**.

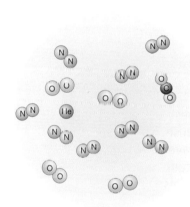

■ Air is a mixture of elements and compounds

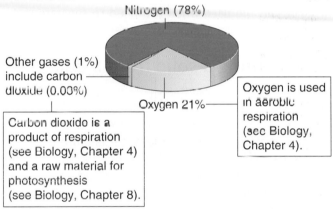

Nitrogen (78%)

Other gases (1%) include carbon dioxide (0.03%)

Carbon dioxide is a product of respiration (see Biology, Chapter 4) and a raw material for photosynthesis (see Biology, Chapter 8).

Oxygen 21%

Oxygen is used in aerobic respiration (see Biology, Chapter 4).

■ Proportions of different elements and compounds in air

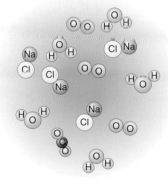

■ Seawater is also a mixture but its elements and compounds are different from those in air

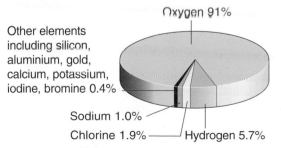

Oxygen 91%

Other elements including silicon, aluminium, gold, calcium, potassium, iodine, bromine 0.4%

Sodium 1.0%

Chlorine 1.9%

Hydrogen 5.7%

■ Proportions of different elements and compounds in seawater

What is separation?

It is often necessary to separate the different materials in a mixture. We usually want to do this because one material is very useful for a particular reason (getting pure drinking water out of seawater, for example). There are many ways in which you can separate the different materials in mixtures; all of these methods depend on some difference between the materials in the mixture. The sort of questions a chemist might ask before trying to carry out a separation would include:

- Do all the materials have the same solubility?
- Do all of the materials have the same boiling point?
- Are some of the materials solid while the others are liquid?
- Do any of the materials have some special physical property that none of the others has?

We have already seen that iron can be separated from other elements because it is magnetic. This is an unusual method of separation. Usually other methods are used when you need to separate materials from a mixture. We will learn about these other methods in the following sections.

Separating a solid from a liquid

Decanting

In many parts of the world, drinking water is collected from the nearest river in large jars. Sometimes the water is quite muddy or sandy because there are particles floating in it. The people who collect the water leave the jars to stand to allow the mud, sand and silt to settle at the bottom of the jar. The clear water can then be poured off and the solid materials will be left behind at the bottom of the jar. This is called **decanting**.

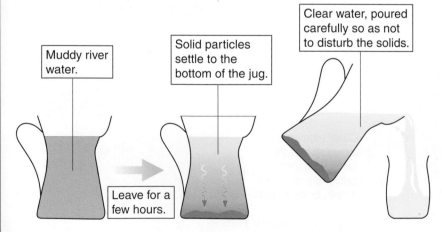

Muddy river water.

Solid particles settle to the bottom of the jug.

Clear water, poured carefully so as not to disturb the solids.

Leave for a few hours.

> Try it yourself. If you leave a carton of orange juice overnight, all the 'bits' of orange settle to the bottom. Pour it carefully next morning and you'll get a clearer liquid on top!

It is very difficult to separate the solid and liquid completely by decanting. To complete the separation of the solid and liquid, it is necessary to use a filter.

Filtration

A **filter** is a layer with many tiny holes in it. The tiny holes let the liquid through but keep the solid back. A filter is like a very fine sieve, and indeed some filters look just like sieves. Some everyday examples of filters include colanders, which are used to hold back cooked vegetables from the water they were boiled in, or tea strainers that we use to keep tea leaves out of a cup of tea.

The liquid that can pass through a filter is called the **filtrate**. The solid that is kept back by the filter is called the **residue**. Filtering (**filtration**) can separate solids from a liquid.

A colander can separate boiled sprouts from water.

Fruit 'bit' like the stones and the skin

Crushed fruit

Cotton stretched over a bowl

Fruit juice without solid 'bits' in it

A tea strainer keeps tea leaves out of a cup of tea.

■ Some everyday examples of filtration

Many filters are made from paper and these can keep back really small particles of solid. Using filter paper is very important in scientific experiments.

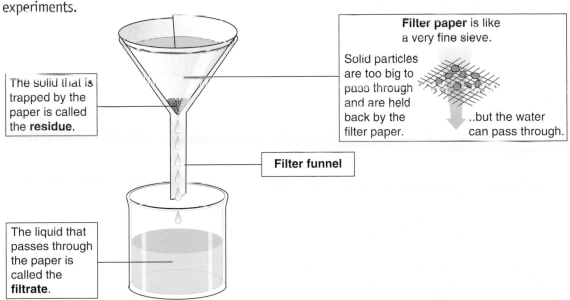

The solid that is trapped by the paper is called the **residue**.

Filter paper is like a very fine sieve.

Solid particles are too big to pass through and are held back by the filter paper.

..but the water can pass through.

Filter funnel

The liquid that passes through the paper is called the **filtrate**.

■ Using filter paper to separate a mixture

43

Separating solids and water: evaporation and crystallisation

We can use filter paper to separate an insoluble substance from a liquid because the particles of the insoluble substance (the solid) are too big to get through the gaps in the filter paper. However, when a substance dissolves in a liquid, the tiny particles of the dissolved substance are so spread out that they can pass through these gaps. This means that you can't use filtration to separate a solute and a solvent.

The way in which you can separate a solute and a solvent is by getting rid of the solvent. You can do this by **evaporation** (the changing of a liquid into a gas).

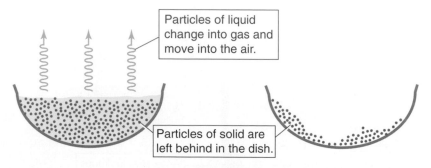

Particles of liquid change into gas and move into the air.

Particles of solid are left behind in the dish.

■ The process of evaporation and crystallisation separates solutes from solvent

If the liquid is water, it is safe to speed up evaporation using a flame.

Never do this with a flammable solvent such as ethanol or propanone.

Evaporation takes place if a liquid is left to stand in a warm place. The process is very much quicker if the solution is gently heated, for example using a low Bunsen flame, but slow evaporation is best if you want to collect crystals of the pure solute.

As the liquid evaporates slowly and the solid dries out, **crystals** form. This process is called **crystallisation** and can produce a pure solid. An example is the formation of copper sulfate crystals from copper sulfate solution.

In the process of crystallisation most of the solvent is removed by heating but then the solution is allowed to cool slowly. This process works because crystals form as the saturated solution cools. Remember that the solubility of a solute falls as the temperature is reduced.

The process of evaporation can be used to show that seawater, tap water and pure water are different from each other (see Chapter 3). Pure water gives no crystals, tap water gives a few but seawater gives many crystals of several different types.

Never heat a solution to the point where it is completely dry. Hot particles of the solvent could spit out and the heat could cause the solute to change in some way.

Filtration and evaporation can be used in the same separation

Sometimes a mixture can be quite complicated. There may be a solvent, a solute and an insoluble substance all together! A mixture like this can be separated into the different substances if two methods, filtration and evaporation, are combined.

One mixture that can be separated by this method is **rock salt**, a mixture of sand and salt (sodium chloride).

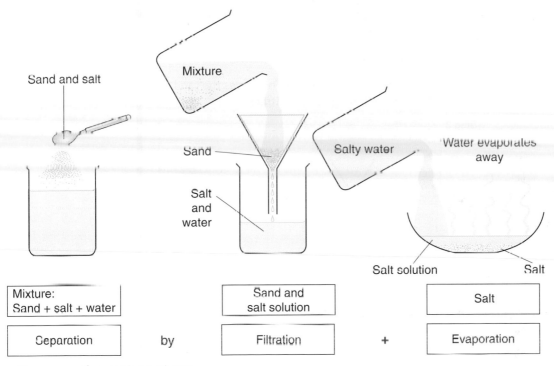

Sand and salt

Mixture

Sand

Salt and water

Salty water

Water evaporates away

Salt solution   Salt

Mixture: Sand + salt + water		Sand and salt solution		Salt
Separation	by	Filtration	+	Evaporation

■ The process of separating a mixture

Working Scientifically

Investigation: Separation of rock salt

The aim of this experiment is to investigate the composition of rock salt by purifying the sample.

The steps in the separation are:

Step 1: Crush the rock salt to make the particles smaller.

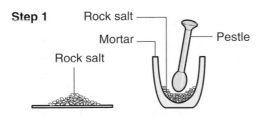

Step 1   Rock salt

Mortar   Pestle

Rock salt

Step 2: Mix the rock salt with water to dissolve the soluble salt.

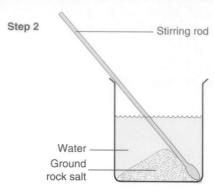

Step 2

Stirring rod

Water

Ground rock salt

Step 3: Pass the mixture through filter paper (filtration). This leaves the sand as a residue and the salt solution passes through as the filtrate.

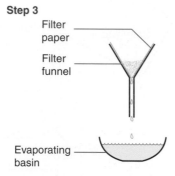

Step 3

Filter paper

Filter funnel

Evaporating basin

Step 4: Warm the salt solution (evaporation). The water evaporates and leaves the salt behind as crystals in the evaporating dish.

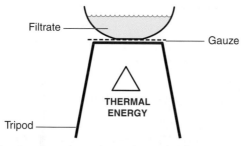

Step 4

Filtrate

Gauze

THERMAL ENERGY

Tripod

Answer the following questions about the procedure.

1 What is the chemical name for common salt?
2 What are the pestle and mortar used for? How does this help in the next step of the separation process?
3 What happens to the material in the rock salt when it is stirred with water? What is the advantage of stirring?
4 The material left in the filter paper is called the **residue**. What material forms the residue here?
5 The **filtrate** is the material that passes through the filter paper. What substance is the filtrate here?

Separation of a solvent from a solution

So we now know that evaporation separates a solute from a solution, but the solvent is usually lost unless special precautions are taken. Sometimes the solvent is valuable and needs to be saved. This can be achieved by evaporating the solvent and then condensing it in a piece of apparatus where the solvent can be collected. The solution is heated, so that the solvent boils quickly and evaporates. This is called **distillation**.

Simple distillation

Simple distillation can be performed using the apparatus shown in the following diagram.

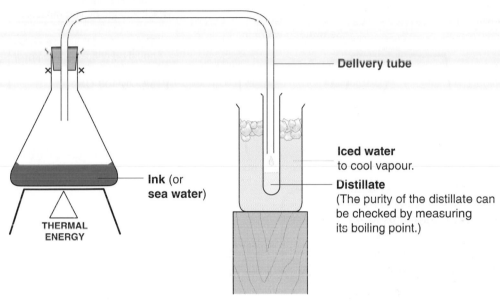

Delivery tube

Iced water
to cool vapour.

Distillate
(The purity of the distillate can be checked by measuring its boiling point.)

Ink (or **sea water**)

THERMAL ENERGY

▨ Using distillation to collect the solvent

Be aware that if the distillate level is allowed to rise up as high as the delivery tube, there could be a problem! If the air in the flask cooled, it would contract and suck pure water back into the ink (or seawater). This is called 'suck-back' and can be prevented by making certain that the delivery tube is always kept above the level of the distillate. The collecting test tube can be moved downwards to make sure that this happens. You must also lift the delivery tube out of the test tube before you stop heating the flask.

The thermal energy used to heat the mixture in this experiment must be controlled quite carefully to ensure that the vapour is only produced at a rate that can be condensed successfully.

Simple distillation can also be performed using the apparatus shown in the next diagram. Here the vapour is directed into a **water-cooled condenser**. This piece of apparatus has a central tube for condensing the solvent and an outer tube that carries cold water. It is more efficient at cooling the vapour than the apparatus shown previously. The condenser is often known as the **Liebig condenser** after the scientist who first worked out how to perform this kind of separation.

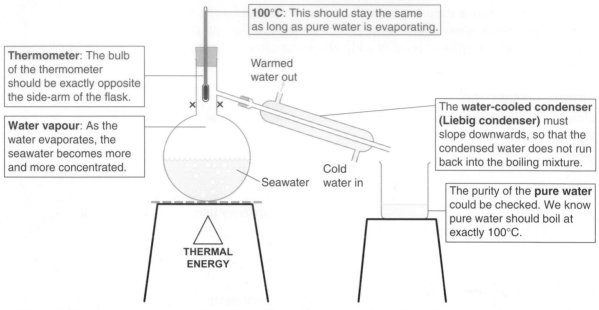

100°C: This should stay the same as long as pure water is evaporating.

Thermometer: The bulb of the thermometer should be exactly opposite the side-arm of the flask.

Warmed water out

The **water-cooled condenser (Liebig condenser)** must slope downwards, so that the condensed water does not run back into the boiling mixture.

Water vapour: As the water evaporates, the seawater becomes more and more concentrated.

Seawater

Cold water in

The purity of the **pure water** could be checked. We know pure water should boil at exactly 100°C.

THERMAL ENERGY

■ Using a Liebig condenser (water-cooled condenser) to condense the pure water from the water vapour

Notice how these diagrams are drawn in cross section. This helps us to see how the apparatus works. From the Liebig condenser diagram we can see that the steam passes through the middle part of the condenser and is cooled by the cold water on the outside.

Did you know?

In Saudi Arabia and other desert countries, drinking water is obtained by distillation of seawater in large desalination plants.

■ An aerial view of a desalination plant

Separation of two liquids from a mixture: fractional distillation

Some liquids, like ethanol and water, mix together. Liquids that mix together in this way are said to be **miscible**. Miscible liquids can be separated as long as they have **different boiling points**. Remember that every pure substance has a fixed boiling point. Ethanol boils at 78 °C and water boils at 100 °C, so when a mixture of the two is heated, the ethanol will evaporate first. Ethanol vapour starts to reach the condenser, cools down and drips into the collecting beaker. Some water does evaporate from the mixture but the cool glass beads in the fractionating column turn the water vapour back to liquid, which trickles back into the flask. If the temperature is kept at 78 °C, almost pure ethanol can be collected. This process is called fractional distillation.

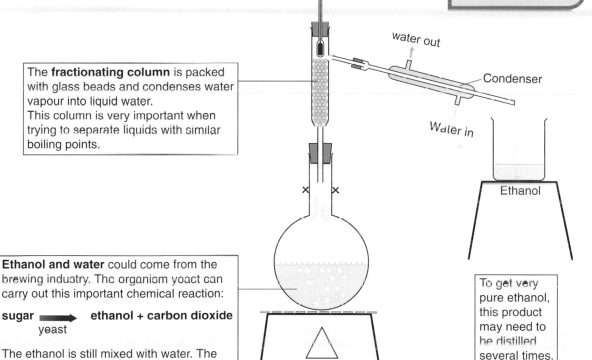

The **fractionating column** is packed with glass beads and condenses water vapour into liquid water.
This column is very important when trying to separate liquids with similar boiling points.

Thermometer
78 °C

water out

Condenser

Water in

Ethanol

Ethanol and water could come from the brewing industry. The organism yeast can carry out this important chemical reaction:

sugar ⟶ ethanol + carbon dioxide
        yeast

The ethanol is still mixed with water. The maximum ethanol concentration that the yeast can survive is about 12% ethanol : 88% water. To make ethanol more concentrated, it must be distilled.

THERMAL ENERGY

To get very pure ethanol, this product may need to be distilled several times.

■ Fractional distillation can be used to separate ethanol from beer or wine

◯ Separation of several different soluble substances: chromatography

Chromatography can be used to separate mixtures of different soluble substances. This process depends on substances having **different solubilities** in a certain solvent. The process is also affected by how much the substances stick to the paper used in the separation. The method for separating a mixture of coloured inks is shown in the following diagram.

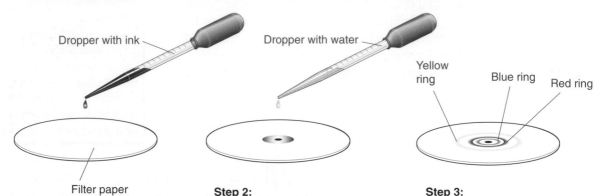

Step 1:
Place a drop of black ink at the centre of a piece of filter paper and let it dry.

Step 2:
Carefully squeeze small drops of water onto the ink. Leave a little time between drops to let the ink spread out. As the water moves across the filter paper, it will carry the colours with it. However, what you will see is that different colours travel at different speeds.

Step 3:
In this ink there are three coloured substances: blue, red and yellow. Notice that the blue dye didn't move as fast as the others. It got left behind and so formed its own ring. Next the red stopped moving. The yellow substance was the most soluble and so moved the furthest.

■ Using water as a solvent in simple paper chromatography

Chromatography can identify unknown substances in a mixture

Chromatography can be used to identify unknown substances in a mixture. Look at the experiment that follows.

- A spot of the mixture is placed on a baseline drawn on a piece of chromatography paper. The baseline must be drawn in pencil, or any colours in the baseline ink will interfere with the result!
- A separating solvent is placed in a jar and the sample paper is allowed to stand in the solvent, until the solvent nears the top of the paper.
- The separating solvent runs up through the paper and pulls the different substances from the spot. The most soluble substance travels furthest up the paper and the least soluble substance travels the shortest distance. Each different dye in the coloured mixture will form a spot in a different place.
- The unknown spots can be compared with spots of known substances so that the unknown materials can be identified.

At the start

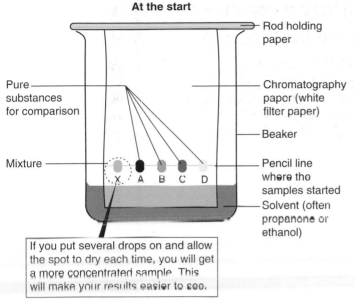

Pure substances for comparison

Mixture

Rod holding paper

Chromatography paper (white filter paper)

Beaker

Pencil line where the samples started

Solvent (often propanone or ethanol)

If you put several drops on and allow the spot to dry each time, you will get a more concentrated sample. This will make your results easier to see.

After the solvent has soaked up the paper

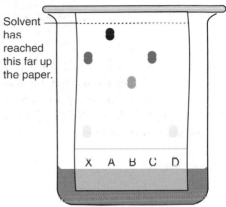

Solvent has reached this far up the paper.

■ Using chromatography to identify unknown substances in a mixture

From the results, we can see that sample X was a mixture of pure substances C and D. We can tell this because it formed two spots of colour: the yellow travelled the same distance as D and the blue travelled the same distance as C.

Investigation: Food colourings chromatography

The aim of this experiment is to see how you can separate and identify mixtures of different soluble substances.

You will be supplied with three food colourings that are labelled A, B and C. Although they are all the same colour, only two of the food colourings contain the same dyes.

Set up the apparatus as shown below:

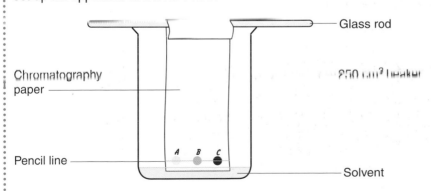

Glass rod

Chromatography paper

250 cm³ beaker

Pencil line

Solvent

Working Scientifically

- Draw a pencil line 1 cm from the bottom of the chromatography paper.
- Use separate glass capillary tubes to place a small drop of each of colours A, B and C on the line and label them in pencil. Alternatively, you can dip the end of a stirring rod or pipette into the solutions and dab them onto the paper.
- Place a small amount of solvent in the bottom of the beaker.
- Hang the chromatography paper into the beaker by wrapping it round a plastic rod so that the solvent is below the pencil line.
- Allow the solvent to rise up the paper until it is almost at the top.
- Hang the chromatogram to dry.
1 When dry, determine which two dyes are the same. What is the reason for your choices?
2 Water is the solvent most commonly used for these separations. Name one other solvent you have studied. Give an example of when this solvent would be used.

Other solvents in chromatography

Some mixtures are not soluble in water, so other solvents must be used to separate them by chromatography. Two important solvents used in this way are **propanone** and **ethanol**. Chromatography is not only used for checking the dyes in different inks, it is also important in:

- checking the sugars in different kinds of foods
- identifying different parts of the blood, including tests on blood at crime scenes
- comparing the pigments (colours) in different types of flowers and leaves.

Exercise 5.1: Separating mixtures

1 Copy and complete these paragraphs, using words from the list below:

> **physical, evaporation, alcohol, boiling points,
> bonded, mixtures, chromatography, pure water**

(a) Most natural substances are _____, they are not pure. The particles of each substance in a mixture are not _____ to each other and so these substances can often be separated because they have different _____ properties.

(b) There are several different ways of separating substances, including _____, which can separate different soluble substances in a mixture and _____, which can provide pure crystals of a solute from a solution.

(c) The process of distillation depends on the fact that different substances have different _____. The process can be used to collect _____ from seawater and _____ from beer or wine.

2 Freddie has a motorcycle and he likes to clean it in his garage.
   (a) After cleaning the motorcycle, he sweeps the floor of the garage so that it is tidy for next time. The sweepings contain iron filings, aluminium shavings, salt and sand. Explain how the different substances in the sweepings could be separated from each other.
   (b) Freddie noticed some liquid on the floor. He thought that it was probably just water, but wanted to check that it wasn't fluid leaking from his brakes. Describe one test he could do to check whether the liquid was just water.

3 Gena loves Smarties. She wanted to look at the colourings used to give the colour to the different sweets, so she tested different coloured Smarties and compared her results with a similar test she did on some artificial colourings, identified with E-numbers. The results of both tests are shown

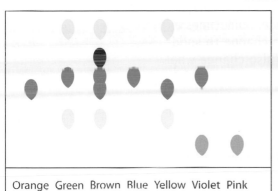

Orange Green Brown Blue Yellow Violet Pink

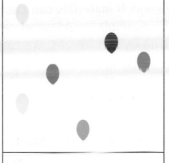

E104 E110 E120 E122 E133

   (a) What is this method of separation called?
   (b) Which colours contain more than one colouring?
   (c) How many of the 'E'-numbered colourings are there in brown Smarties?
   (d) Gena is sensitive to E110 (it makes her hyperactive). Which colours of Smarties must she avoid?

6 Material changes

Scientists now understand that everything in the Universe is made of up of atoms and molecules. These atoms and molecules can have useful properties. However, it doesn't stop there: materials can also change from one kind of material to another. If their properties are really useful, then humans may deliberately make materials change.

There are many ways in which materials can change. Sometimes a material changes state, for example liquid water can change to solid water (ice) when it cools down and freezes. We can also change what a material is, for example burning a match changes it from wood into ash, water vapour and a gas called carbon dioxide.

Scientists can put these changes into different groups. One way of grouping these changes is suggested here:

- changes that happen when materials are **mixed** with one another (for example, stirring sugar into tea)
- changes that happen when materials are **heated** or **cooled** (for example, cooking bread from dough)
- changes that result in the **formation of new materials** (for example, a nail going rusty; see more about oxidation in the section on 'Burning' in Chapter 7).

This system is not ideal, however, as some changes might overlap between two groups and that can be confusing! You can make new materials by mixing two materials together **and** heating them, for example. So perhaps these three groups are not very good because there are too many overlaps.

Another way of grouping these changes could be as follows:

- changes that **can be reversed** (such as melting chocolate to liquid and then letting it cool down again)
- changes that **cannot be reversed** (for example, cooking an egg; once the egg is cooked, we cannot change it back into an uncooked egg).

This way of grouping the changes is better, but we need more information.

Physical and chemical changes

As we have seen, there are several ways that changes to materials can be grouped. However, the most useful one that scientists have come up with is the one that separates **physical changes** from **chemical changes**. This system works as there is little overlap between the groups. Let's look at these changes in more detail.

■ Comparing physical and chemical changes

Physical changes	Chemical changes
These are changes in the way in which a material looks and feels.	These are changes where the material breaks down completely.
These changes are temporary and can be reversed.	Normally these changes are permanent and they cannot be reversed.
No new materials are formed in physical changes.	New materials are formed as a result of these chemical changes.

> You will learn more about chemical changes in Chapter 7.

Exercise 6.1: Changing materials

1 Copy the table and complete the second column by saying whether each change is a physical or a chemical change. Write a reason for your choice in the third column.

Diagram	Physical or chemical change?	Reason
1 A melting ice cream		
2 Burning a match		
3 Making bread from dough		
4 Stirring sugar into a cup of tea		
5 Condensation on a mirror		
6 Mercury rising in a thermometer		
7 Burning a piece of paper		
8 Making glass from sand		
9 Making alcohol		
10 Melting gold		

Physical changes and conservation of mass

Physical changes cause the particles of a substance to be rearranged. No chemical bonds are formed, and no particles are lost or gained.

If no particles are lost or gained, there should be no change in the mass of a substance when it goes through a physical change. This is called **conservation of mass**.

Conservation of mass during a change of state

If you measure an exact mass of water, freeze it, take its mass, then thaw it out, you will find that the freezing and thawing have had no effect on the mass of the water.

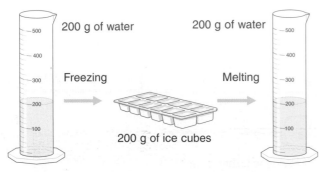

So remember, when a change of state takes place, the mass before the change is equal to the mass after the change. This is because the number of particles stays the same.

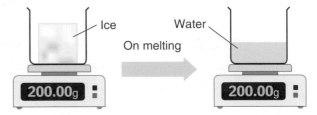

Conservation of mass during mixing and separation

If you add 10 g of sugar to a dish of water and stir the two substances together, the sugar will dissolve and become invisible. You can collect the sugar again by allowing the water to evaporate away. At the end of this experiment you will find that there is still 10 g of sugar.

This is because the total mass of the solution is equal to the mass of the solute plus the mass of solvent. In theory, the same mass of solute and solvent should be recoverable on separation – although in practice it would be very difficult to do so exactly.

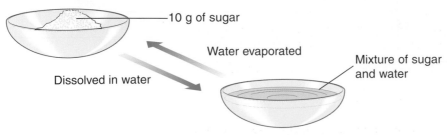

The law of conservation of mass applies to **all** physical changes.

Investigation: What happens to a solute when a solution is formed?

The aim of this experiment is to investigate what happens to the mass of a solute when a solution is formed.

- Check that your balance is set to zero.
- Use the balance to measure out about 5 g of sodium chloride (common salt) as accurately as possible into a specimen tube. Record the mass.
- Pour some water into a beaker, until it is about half-full.
- Again check that the balance is set to zero. Find the mass of the beaker of water.
- Remove the beaker from the balance and add the sodium chloride to the water.
- **Predict** what the final mass will be.
- Place the beaker onto the balance and record the mass of the beaker and the solution.

1 When a solution is formed what happens to the mass?
2 Everything is made of particles. The particles in a solid can only vibrate but the particles in a liquid can move about. What do you think happens to the particles in the liquid and in the solid when a solution is formed?
3 Imagine that you can use a 'particleiser' to see the particles in the beaker. Draw your ideas. Use colour coding to show the different particles.
4 From the evidence you have collected, complete the following statement: The mass of a solution is equal to ...

Exercise 6.2: Conservation of mass

1 What would be the mass of ice cubes formed from 200 ml of water?
   Hint: Remember that 1 ml of water weighs 1 g.
2 Sarah carried out two experiments:
   (a) **Experiment 1:**
       Sarah mixed 81 g of sodium iodide solution with 75 g of silver nitrate solution. A yellow precipitate formed in the solution.
       Sarah separated the solid from the solution by filtration into a conical flask, and measured the mass of the solid. There was 3 g of solid on the filter paper.
       (i) What was the mass of solution in the conical flask?
       (ii) What would the total mass of products be if Sarah had started with 105 g of sodium iodide solution and 111 g of silver nitrate solution?
   (b) **Experiment 2:**
       Sarah added solid calcium carbonate to sulfuric acid in a beaker. The reaction between these two compounds can be shown in the equation:

Calcium carbonate + sulfuric acid → calcium sulfate + carbon dioxide + water

       (i) State one way in which Sarah knew that a chemical reaction had taken place.
       (ii) The total mass of the beaker and its contents was less at the end of the experiment than it was at the beginning. Explain why.

7 Chemical reactions

Everything that we use is made of materials. These materials are chemicals. Each material has properties that might make it useful to humans.

Properties of materials may be altered by **non-reversible chemical changes** (see Chapter 6), also referred to as **chemical reactions**. Chemical reactions result in the formation of new materials. Almost all materials are made through chemical reactions; this means that chemical changes are extremely important in everyday life.

Some materials are obviously made by humans, such as concrete, plastics, medicines, fertilisers and detergents. Other materials are made by 'natural' chemical reactions. For example, oxygen in the air and starches in plants are made by photosynthesis.

A chemical reaction:

- has starting materials called **reactants**
- creates new materials called **products**
- always involves an **energy change**
- is **difficult to reverse.**

How to recognise a chemical reaction

There are definite signs that we can look for to check whether a chemical reaction has occurred.

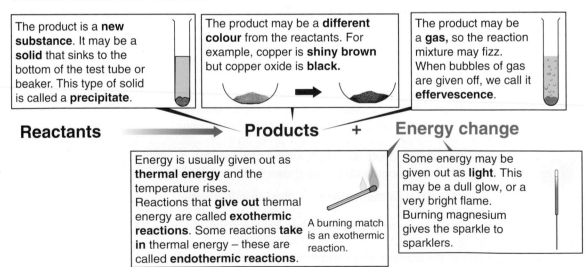

The product is a **new substance**. It may be a **solid** that sinks to the bottom of the test tube or beaker. This type of solid is called a **precipitate**.

The product may be a **different colour** from the reactants. For example, copper is **shiny brown** but copper oxide is **black.**

The product may be a **gas,** so the reaction mixture may fizz. When bubbles of gas are given off, we call it **effervescence.**

Reactants ⟶ **Products** + **Energy change**

Energy is usually given out as **thermal energy** and the temperature rises.
Reactions that **give out** thermal energy are called **exothermic reactions**. Some reactions **take in** thermal energy – these are called **endothermic reactions**.

A burning match is an exothermic reaction.

Some energy may be given out as **light**. This may be a dull glow, or a very bright flame. Burning magnesium gives the sparkle to sparklers.

■ How to spot a chemical change: the reactants will be changed and difficult to reverse

The type of apparatus shown in the following diagram can be used to observe some chemical reactions.

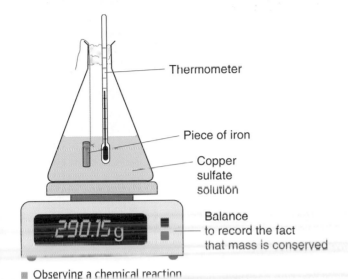

- Thermometer
- Piece of iron
- Copper sulfate solution
- Balance to record the fact that mass is conserved

■ Observing a chemical reaction

Did you know?
Explosions are exothermic reactions that usually give out a great deal of light and sound!

Describing chemical reactions

Chemical reactions can be described by **word equations**. Word equations are like short sentences that describe chemical reactions. In a word equation:

- we list the reactants first and then the products
- we change some of the words from the sentence into symbols, to save space: the '+' sign means 'and'; an arrow ($\rightarrow$) means 'changed into'.

  reactants $\rightarrow$ products

  Here are some examples of word equations:
- The burning of carbon in oxygen:

  carbon + oxygen $\rightarrow$ carbon dioxide

- The reaction between iron and sulfur:

  iron + sulfur $\rightarrow$ iron sulfide

Many chemical changes are useful to humans; however there are some that are not useful. Whether a chemical reaction is useful or not, it is important that scientists work out how it might be controlled. Science allows us to understand how chemical reactions take place; once we understand what is happening in a chemical change, we might be able to control it, so that it suits our human purpose. It is, however, important that we always consider how these reactions might affect the world around us.

Working Scientifically

Some substances do **not** change chemically when heated. Copper oxide (which is black) and magnesium oxide (which is a white powder, as long as it has been previously heated in an oven to remove water) do not change colour when they are heated strongly, and no gases are released. These observations suggest that no chemical change has taken place.

Did you know?
Zinc oxide (which is white) does change colour when it is heated (it turns yellow). However it returns to white again when it cools. Weighing it before and after heating shows that no chemical reaction has taken place. The colour change is instead due to the change in the way light is reflected, due to the energy of particles.

Exercise 7.1: Chemical changes

1 Write down two things that you might **see** when a chemical change takes place.

2 Write down two things that you might **hear** when a chemical change takes place.

3 Read this description of a chemical reaction demonstrated by a teacher:
A small quantity of the metal sodium was placed into a gas jar containing green chlorine gas until a dirty-white solid was formed. Although the reaction was slow to start, eventually a lot of thermal energy was given out.
(a) Write out a word equation for the reaction that has taken place.
(b) Give three reasons why you believe a chemical reaction has taken place.

4 Maria wanted to investigate the differences between physical and chemical changes. She put three chemicals in separate crucibles and weighed each one. She then heated each crucible. She weighed each crucible again when it had cooled down. She recorded her observations in a table as shown below.

Working Scientifically

Experiment	Name of chemical	Observations	Change in mass
A	Magnesium (a silvery solid)	The silvery magnesium burned brightly in air. A white powder was formed.	Increase
B	Potassium manganate(VII) (purple crystals)	The purple crystals crackled and turned black. A colourless gas was given off.	Decrease
C	Zinc oxide (a white powder)	The white powder turned pale yellow on heating. It turned white again on cooling.	No change

(a) (i) In experiment A, magnesium reacts with a gas in the air. Copy and complete the word equation for the reaction:
magnesium + _____ → _____

(ii) Explain the increase in mass in experiment A. Use your word equation to help you.
(b) The gas given off in experiment B relit a glowing splint. Give the name of this gas.
(c) Name the white powder left at the end of experiment C.
(d) For each experiment, A, B and C, state whether a chemical change or a physical change has taken place.

Useful chemical reactions

Scientists and technologists have discovered that there are many reactions that are useful to humans. The diagram below illustrates some of these.

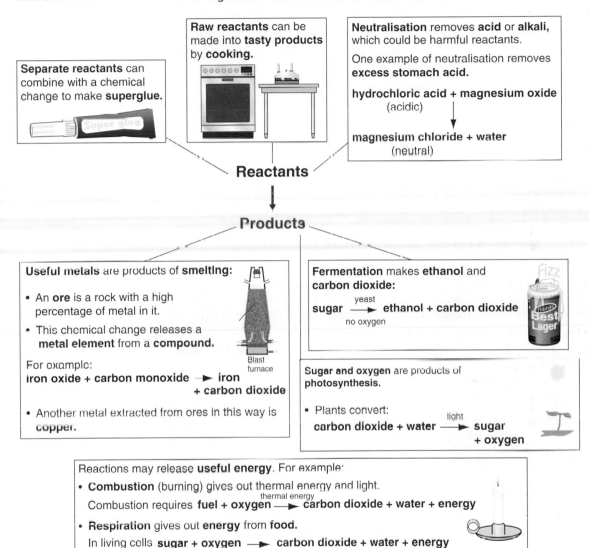

Separate reactants can combine with a chemical change to make **superglue**.

Raw reactants can be made into **tasty products** by **cooking**.

Neutralisation removes **acid** or **alkali**, which could be harmful reactants.

One example of neutralisation removes **excess stomach acid**.

hydrochloric acid + magnesium oxide
(acidic)

↓

magnesium chloride + water
(neutral)

Reactants

↓

Products

Useful metals are products of **smelting**:

• An **ore** is a rock with a high percentage of metal in it.

• This chemical change releases a **metal element** from a **compound**.

For example:
iron oxide + carbon monoxide ➝ iron + carbon dioxide

Blast furnace

• Another metal extracted from ores in this way is **copper**.

Fermentation makes **ethanol** and **carbon dioxide**:

$$\text{sugar} \xrightarrow[\text{no oxygen}]{\text{yeast}} \text{ethanol + carbon dioxide}$$

fizz

Best Lager

Sugar and oxygen are products of **photosynthesis**.

• Plants convert:
$$\text{carbon dioxide + water} \xrightarrow{\text{light}} \text{sugar + oxygen}$$

Reactions may release **useful energy**. For example:

• **Combustion** (burning) gives out thermal energy and light.
Combustion requires **fuel + oxygen** $\xrightarrow{\text{thermal energy}}$ **carbon dioxide + water + energy**

• **Respiration** gives out **energy** from **food**.
In living cells **sugar + oxygen** ➝ **carbon dioxide + water + energy**

■ Chemical reactions can make useful products

Some of these useful reactions are explained in more detail in other parts of this book. However, it is worth just summarising them here before we move on.

● **Combustion** gives out **energy**. This energy can be used for heating homes, factories and hospitals, for example. It can also be used for making other chemicals react together or for generating electricity. Combustion only goes on if oxygen is present (see later in this chapter).

- **Neutralisation** involves the removal of acid or alkali because these substances may be harmful (see Chapter 8).
- **Smelting** is the extraction of metals from ores. This provides us with purified metals that have many important properties and uses (see Chapter 8).
- **Fermentation** is the production of alcohol (and carbon dioxide). This chemical reaction only goes on properly if no oxygen is present and was one of the earliest chemical reactions that humans used.
- **Photosynthesis** is the production of sugar and oxygen using light energy. This process is the start of all the food chains in nature: no food chains, no humans (see Chapter 8 in Biology).
- **Respiration** is the process that releases energy from food molecules inside our cells. This energy is used to keep all of the life processes going. Without this chemical reaction, there would be no living things (see Chapter 4 in Biology).
- **Cooking food** makes it safer, tastier and easier to eat. Molecules in the food are changed during cooking. For example, frying an egg alters proteins and fats in the egg so that the cooked egg has products that are more solid and taste different from those in a raw egg.

- **Glues and adhesives** work by forming a bond between different materials. Some glues stick because different substances in the glue react together. Superglue works because the molecules of glue change the way in which they are arranged (they become much more sticky) when they contact **moisture** or **alkali.** This is why this type of glue is sometimes called **contact adhesive**.

Ethanol is a poison. It will eventually kill the yeast cells that produce it and it does the same to human cells if taken in too large a quantity.

Fermentation is a chemical reaction.
- We can tell which are reactants and which are products.
- The arrow shows the direction of change.
- New substances are produced and there is an energy change.
- The process cannot be reversed.

This **energy** is needed by the yeast to carry out its life processes. The yeast cells reproduce using this energy, so some yeast cells may remain in the bottle.

glucose ➡ **ethanol + carbon dioxide + energy**

Glucose (sugar) is the reactant. This substance comes from a fruit (e.g. grapes in wine production) or a seed (e.g. malt in beer production).

Did you know?

Fermentation can only produce a mixture of ethanol and water. Distillation (see Chapter 5) is needed to purify the ethanol. Stronger alcoholic drinks called spirits, such as gin, whisky and brandy, are made from distillation.

Ethanol is important in brewing

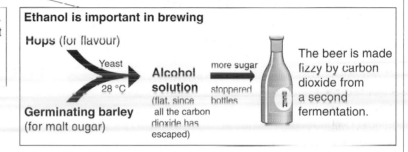

Hops (for flavour)

Yeast

28 °C

Germinating barley (for malt sugar)

Alcohol solution (flat, since all the carbon dioxide has escaped)

more sugar ➡ stoppered bottles

The beer is made fizzy by carbon dioxide from a second fermentation.

Carbon dioxide is especially important in bread making

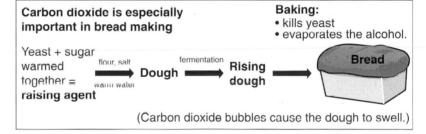

Yeast + sugar warmed together = **raising agent**

flour, salt ➡ warm water

Dough ➡ (fermentation) **Rising dough** ➡ **Bread**

Baking:
- kills yeast
- evaporates the alcohol.

(Carbon dioxide bubbles cause the dough to swell.)

■ Important uses of fermentation

◯ Chemical reactions that are not useful

Many materials can take part in chemical reactions, although some materials are much less reactive than others. Sometimes these materials are useful as they are and it is a nuisance if they change into something else. Some chemical reactions result in products that may cause damage or harm. Some 'non-useful' chemical reactions are shown in the diagram on the next page.

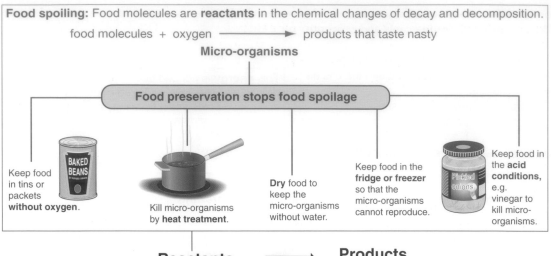

Food spoiling: Food molecules are **reactants** in the chemical changes of decay and decomposition.

food molecules + oxygen ⟶ products that taste nasty

Micro-organisms

Food preservation stops food spoilage

Keep food in tins or packets **without oxygen**.

Kill micro-organisms by **heat treatment**.

Dry food to keep the micro-organisms without water.

Keep food in the **fridge or freezer** so that the micro-organisms cannot reproduce.

Keep food in the **acid conditions**, e.g. vinegar to kill micro-organisms.

Reactants ⟶ **Products**

Corrosion converts useful metal into a damaged product (see Chapter 8).
- The process is called **oxidation**. It uses oxygen from air or water.

  metal + oxygen ⟶ metal oxide

- **Metal oxide** is weaker and softer than the metal, so corroded objects break easily.

- The most important example of corrosion is **rusting**.

Pollution is caused by **products** of chemical reactions which take place in industry.

Acid rain:
- Combustion of fuels produces **oxides of sulfur and nitrogen.**
- Oxides react with the water in clouds to make **acid rain.**
- Acid rain irritates our lungs and eyes, damages leaves on trees and dissolves some building materials.

Greenhouse effect:
- Carbon dioxide is a **product** of burning fossil fuels.
- Methane is a **product** of cows' digestion of grass.
- These gases trap warm air close to the Earth's surface.

Melting of ice caps – bad news for penguins!

■ Some chemical changes cause damage or danger

This list gives a summary of these reactions and tells you where you can find out more about them:

1 **Decay** and **decomposition** are processes that break down other materials. This includes the rotting or spoiling of food and some diseases. When food rots it reacts with oxygen in the air to form new compounds that taste unpleasant; we say that the food is **rancid.** This happens most often with foods that contain fat, so foods such as cheese and crisps are often sealed up in bags filled with nitrogen. Because there is no oxygen in the bags, the fats are

not oxidised and the food is **preserved.** Some foods rot because micro-organisms called **decomposers** use the food molecules to carry out the chemical reactions they need to stay alive (see Biology, Chapter 8).

2 **Corrosion** is the oxidation of metals. This includes rusting, which damages many structures and buildings (see Chapter 8).

3 **Acid rain** is formed from the products of burning fossil fuels. It can cause damage to buildings, trees and your lungs (see Chapter 8).

4 The **greenhouse effect** is caused by certain gases that trap thermal (internal) energy close to the Earth's surface. One way in which these gases are produced is by the combustion of fossil fuels (see 'Using fuels' later in this chapter).

■ Rotting and mouldy tomatoes

Exercise 7.2: Important chemical changes

1 A baker wanted to try out a new dough mix. He needed to know how long it would take to swell to a certain size. (Dough needs to swell, or 'prove', before bread is baked in the oven.)

He made up a sample of the dough and dropped it into a measuring cylinder, as shown in the diagram. He left the dough standing on a radiator and went back to check it every five minutes for half an hour.

Working Scientifically

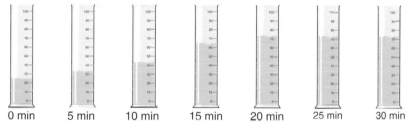

| 0 min | 5 min | 10 min | 15 min | 20 min | 25 min | 30 min |

(Start of experiment)

Estimate the height of the dough shown in the measuring cylinders and record the baker's results in a table like the one below. Then answer the questions on the next page.

Time/minutes	Volume of dough/cm³
0	
5	
10	
15	
20	
25	
30	

(a) Draw a line graph to show how the amount of dough changed over the half-hour period.

(b) Use your graph to work out how long he would need to leave the dough for it to swell to twice its original size.

(c) The baker decided to try to find out how much the amount of sugar in the dough affected the volume of the dough.

    (i) What would be the **independent** (input) variable in this experiment?

    (ii) What would be the **dependent** (outcome) variable in this experiment?

    (iii) Give two important variables the baker would need to control for this experiment to be a fair test. Explain how these variables could be checked.

2 Give two examples of useful chemical reactions that occur naturally and two examples of natural chemical reactions that are not useful.

3 Make a list of ten substances that you could find at home. Pick out which of the substances have been made by a chemical reaction. Choose one substance from your list and find out which reactants were needed to make it.

◯ Conservation of mass during chemical changes

All chemicals are made up of particles (see Chapter 1). During a chemical reaction these particles are rearranged into a new pattern **but they are never broken down**.

When a mix of iron (Fe) and sulfur (S) is heated, iron sulfide (FeS) is formed. Each particle of iron reacts with one particle of sulfur.

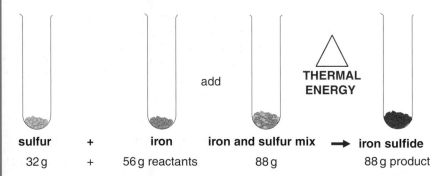

sulfur	+	iron	iron and sulfur mix	→	iron sulfide
32 g	+	56 g reactants	88 g		88 g product

The particle theory explains why, during any chemical reaction, there is **conservation of mass**. This means the total mass of the reactants used is the same as the total mass of the products formed.

The following diagram shows a demonstration of the conservation of mass during a chemical change.

> Remember that the conservation of mass also applies to physical changes (see Chapter 6, 'Physical changes and conservation of mass').

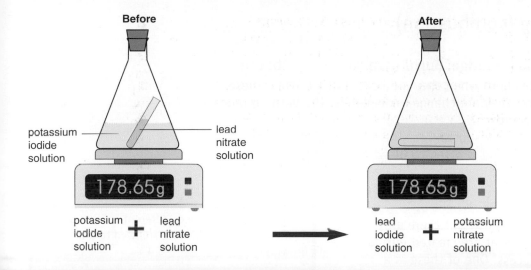

Before — After

potassium iodide solution / lead nitrate solution

178.65 g   178.65 g

potassium iodide solution **+** lead nitrate solution $\longrightarrow$ lead iodide solution **+** potassium nitrate solution

Exercise 7.3: Conservation of mass

1 Look at the diagram. It shows an experiment where magnesium ribbon is burned in air.

Step 1: Before heating, weigh the magnesium ribbon, crucible and lid.

Step 2: Heat the ribbon strongly.

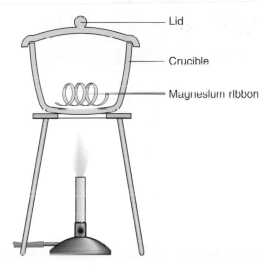

Lid

Crucible

Magnesium ribbon

Never watch magnesium burning. The bright light can damage your eyes unless you look through a protective blue filter.

Step 3: After heating, weigh the magnesium oxide and crucible lid.

The following results were obtained:

Mass of crucible	50 g
Mass of crucible + magnesium ribbon	62 g
Mass of crucible + contents after heating	70 g

Explain these results.

Burning (combustion)

Preliminary knowledge: Burning makes new substances

Some substances burn when they are heated in air. When these substances burn, they are changed completely. The burning process **cannot be reversed**.

Burning makes new substances. The substance that burns is called the fuel, and is often changed into another solid material (ash).

Burning is a chemical change

It is easy to see the ash but there are other substances that are created during the burning process. One of these is a gas, called carbon dioxide, and the other is water.

Burning is a chemical change called combustion.

- Combustion needs **thermal energy** (heat) to get it started.
- Combustion is a chemical reaction in which thermal energy and **light energy** are produced.
- During combustion, oxygen from the air combines with another element to form an oxide. This is a type of oxidation reaction.

Burning metals produces different colours of light energy. The following are used to make fireworks:

- magnesium gives a bright, white light
- calcium gives a red, sparkling light.

■ A firework display at the 2012 London Olympics

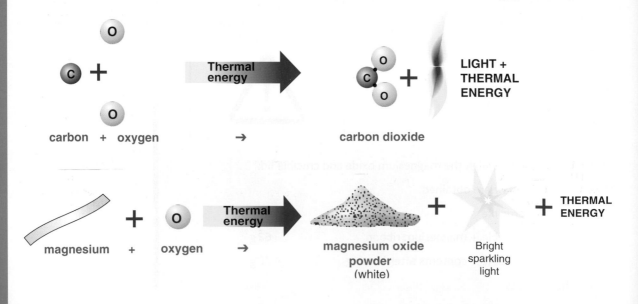

carbon + oxygen → carbon dioxide

Thermal energy

LIGHT + THERMAL ENERGY

magnesium + oxygen → magnesium oxide powder (white)

Thermal energy

Bright sparkling light

+ THERMAL ENERGY

Products of burning

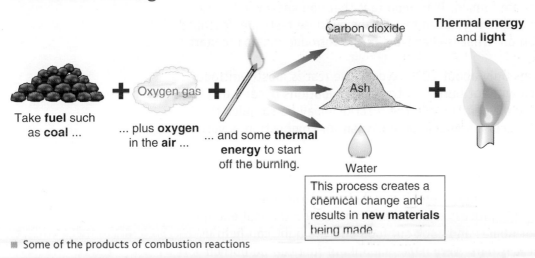

Take **fuel** such as **coal** ...

... plus **oxygen** in the **air** ...

... and some **thermal energy** to start off the burning.

Carbon dioxide

Ash

Water

Thermal energy and **light**

This process creates a chemical change and results in **new materials** being made.

■ Some of the products of combustion reactions

Some thermal energy is needed to get things going; even a match has to be rubbed against a matchbox before it will catch light.

However, the thermal energy given out by burning is always more than the thermal energy needed to start it off.

The following diagram shows the products of the burning reaction with the word equation:

$$\text{hydrocarbon} + \text{oxygen} \rightarrow \text{water} + \text{carbon dioxide}$$
$$\text{(from fuel)} \quad \text{(from air)}$$

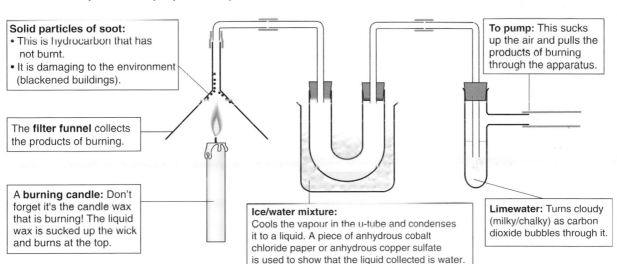

Solid particles of soot:
• This is hydrocarbon that has not burnt.
• It is damaging to the environment (blackened buildings).

The **filter funnel** collects the products of burning.

A **burning candle:** Don't forget it's the candle wax that is burning! The liquid wax is sucked up the wick and burns at the top.

To pump: This sucks up the air and pulls the products of burning through the apparatus.

Ice/water mixture:
Cools the vapour in the u-tube and condenses it to a liquid. A piece of anhydrous cobalt chloride paper or anhydrous copper sulfate is used to show that the liquid collected is water.

Limewater: Turns cloudy (milky/chalky) as carbon dioxide bubbles through it.

Combustion is a chemical reaction and when combustion occurs new products are formed. It is important that you know what these products are and how you can test for them. These tests are described in the section on 'What is chemistry' in the Introduction at the start of this book.

Air contains only about 20% oxygen (the rest is mostly nitrogen and materials will not burn in nitrogen). Oxidations occur much more quickly if pure oxygen is used. The reactions may be so quick that an explosion occurs, so using pure oxygen for combustion is very dangerous!

Using fuels

Burning fuels is an important chemical change. The energy that is given out in this process is useful to humans. The thermal energy can warm our homes and cook our food and the light can help us to see when it is dark. Very large amounts of fuel can be burned in power stations. The thermal energy given out can be converted into electricity. Electricity is a more useful kind of energy because we can send it along wires. This means that humans can use even more energy and they can use it in a different place from where it was released. This means that our lives can be cleaner and more convenient.

bad for enviroment

Oil

Gas

Coal

■ Fossil fuels can be burned in power stations to provide electricity to heat and light our homes

Investigation: Burning

The aim of this experiment is to compare the amount of thermal energy produced from different fuels.

Set up the apparatus as shown in the diagram below.

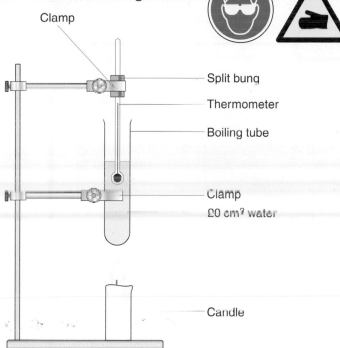

Clamp

Split bung

Thermometer

Boiling tube

Clamp

20 cm³ water

Candle

- Weigh the candle and container, and record their mass in your results table (see below).
- Record the initial temperature of your water in your results table.
- Light the candle and heat the water for approximately 3 minutes.
- Extinguish the candle and leave to cool.
- Record the maximum temperature that the water reaches in your results table.
- Weigh the cooled candle and container, and record their mass in your results table.

	Results
Initial mass of candle + container in grams	
Final mass of candle + container in grams	
Mass of fuel used in grams	
Initial temperature of water in °C	
Final temperature of water in °C	
Temperature rise in °C	

Wash out your boiling tube and repeat the experiment using a spirit burner containing ethanol. Record your results in another column of this results table.

1   To calculate the temperature rise for 1g of fuel, work out the temperature rise of water divided by mass of fuel (units °C/g). This gives a measure of the energy content of these fuels. Which fuel produced more thermal energy?
2   When things burn they combine with oxygen. Why do you think that a candle gets smaller as it burns?

Exercise 7.4: Burning

1   Give a reason why covering burning wood with a blanket will put out a fire.

2   A scientist wanted to find out how much thermal energy is given out when fuels burn. He took different fuels, burned them and measured the thermal energy released. Here are the results:

Type of fuel	Units of thermal energy released	Amount of fuel burned/grams	Units of thermal energy from 100 grams of fuel
Coal	40	60	
Gas	54	80	
Paraffin	36	50	
Petrol	60	50	
Diesel oil	54	75	

(a) Copy out the table. Using the information from the table, calculate the number of units of thermal energy that would be obtained by burning 100 grams of fuel. Use your results to complete the final column.
(b) Why is it important to complete this final column?
(c) The scientist always used the same amount of air for his experiment. Why is this important?
(d) Draw a bar chart of the results from the final column.
(e) Which is the most efficient heating fuel?
(f) Is the most efficient heating fuel the most useful one? If not which fuel is the most useful heating fuel? Give your reasons for your choice.
   Hint: You will need to research and consider cost and storage/delivery factors as well as efficiency.

Combustion and the environment: problems with fossil fuels

As we saw in the previous section, natural gas, coal and oil are called **fossil fuels**. Fossil fuels are substances that were formed millions of years ago from the remains of dead animals and plants. These fuels contain many of the chemicals that were present in the live animals and plants. These chemicals are made up of different elements, including carbon, hydrogen, sulfur and nitrogen.

We have seen that when fuel is burned (combustion), these elements combine with oxygen from the air to make oxides. Because these reactions are all chemical changes, we can write out word equations to describe them.

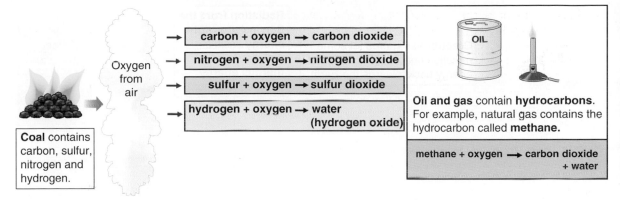

Coal contains carbon, sulfur, nitrogen and hydrogen.

Oxygen from air

carbon + oxygen → carbon dioxide

nitrogen + oxygen → nitrogen dioxide

sulfur + oxygen → sulfur dioxide

hydrogen + oxygen → water (hydrogen oxide)

OIL

Oil and gas contain **hydrocarbons**. For example, natural gas contains the hydrocarbon called **methane**.

methane + oxygen → carbon dioxide + water

■ Burning fossil fuels

Did you know?

If there is too little oxygen present when fossil fuels burn, carbon may react with oxygen to form carbon monoxide (CO) instead of carbon dioxide (CO_2). This gas binds inside the red blood cells and prevents them carrying as much oxygen around the body. This can be fatal. This is why it is important to have your gas boiler inspected regularly and have a carbon monoxide alarm installed.

■ A carbon monoxide alarm for the home

Burning fossil fuels gives out very large amounts of energy, but there are two important problems:

- Fossil fuels are **non-renewable**; in other words they take thousands of years to be made, so once current supplies are used up, there won't be any more available for us to use.
- Fossil fuels cause **pollution**; smoke, ash and waste gases cause damage to our environment, especially to the air. Some of this damage affects humans as well as other living organisms.

The greenhouse effect

The Earth is warmed by **radiation** from the Sun. The radiation reaches the Earth and is then reflected back out towards space. Some of the reflected radiation is **trapped** by the atmosphere. Layers of gases stop this reflected thermal (internal) energy from escaping back into the atmosphere and reflect it back towards the Earth's surface. This is a natural effect and keeps the surface of the Earth at an ideal temperature for life (the average over the Earth's surface is about 16 °C). This effect is very similar to the way in which the glass in a greenhouse lets light energy in but stops thermal (internal) energy from escaping. This is why the layers of gas are called **greenhouse gases**.

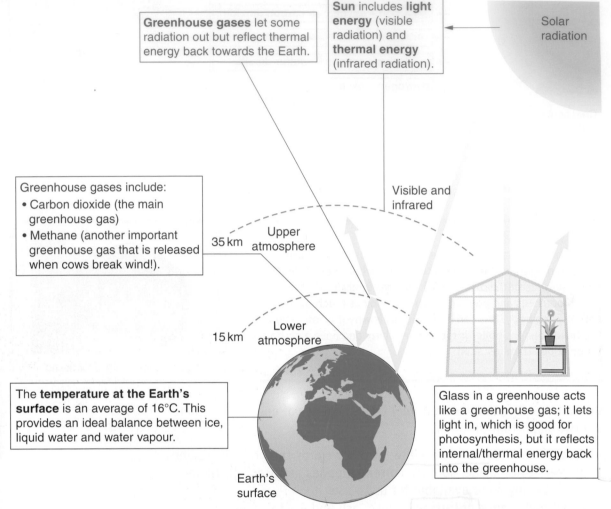

Greenhouse gases let some radiation out but reflect thermal energy back towards the Earth.

Radiation from the Sun includes **light energy** (visible radiation) and **thermal energy** (infrared radiation).

Solar radiation

Visible and infrared

Greenhouse gases include:
• Carbon dioxide (the main greenhouse gas)
• Methane (another important greenhouse gas that is released when cows break wind!).

35 km   Upper atmosphere

15 km   Lower atmosphere

The **temperature at the Earth's surface** is an average of 16°C. This provides an ideal balance between ice, liquid water and water vapour.

Earth's surface

Glass in a greenhouse acts like a greenhouse gas; it lets light in, which is good for photosynthesis, but it reflects internal/thermal energy back into the greenhouse.

■ The greenhouse effect

Burning fossil fuels produces more of these greenhouse gases and so more thermal energy is continually reflected back towards the Earth's surface. This makes the Earth warmer. Scientists have measured the Earth's temperature for hundreds of years and they think that the Earth has become about 2 °C warmer in the last 100 years. This is called **global warming**.

The likely effects of global warming are shown in the following diagram.

Did you know?

Termites produce more methane than all the cows in the world!

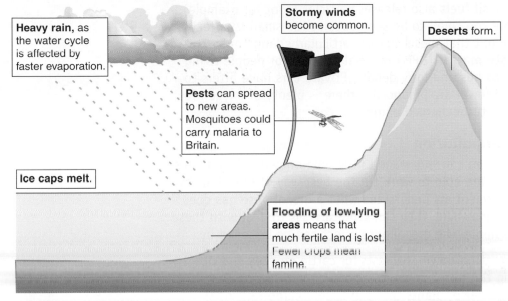

Heavy rain, as the water cycle is affected by faster evaporation.

Stormy winds become common.

Deserts form.

Pests can spread to new areas. Mosquitoes could carry malaria to Britain.

Ice caps melt.

Flooding of low-lying areas means that much fertile land is lost. Fewer crops mean famine.

■ The effects of global warming

Acid rain

As you have learned, combustion produces new products called oxides. Some of these oxides are acid gases (see Chapter 8). One of these acid gases is sulfur dioxide. The acid gases dissolve in water in clouds and form acids. When it rains, these acids fall and land on the Earth. This **acid rain** causes many problems, as you can see in the following diagram.

Carbon dioxide is a weak acid. This means rain is **always** slightly acidic.

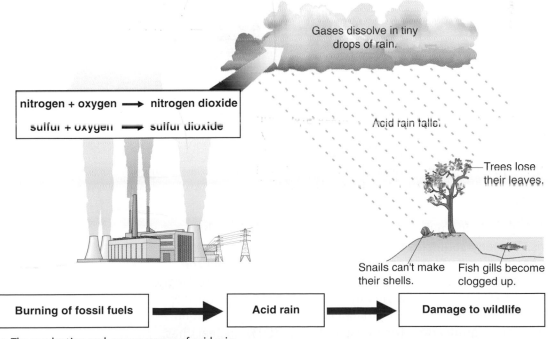

Gases dissolve in tiny drops of rain.

nitrogen + oxygen ⟶ nitrogen dioxide

sulfur + oxygen ⟶ sulfur dioxide

Acid rain falls.

Trees lose their leaves.

Snails can't make their shells.

Fish gills become clogged up.

| Burning of fossil fuels | ⟶ | Acid rain | ⟶ | Damage to wildlife |

■ The production and consequences of acid rain

The burning of fossil fuels also releases particles (soot for example). Some of these are too small to be seen but not too small to affect health. It is thought that diesel fuel is particularly dangerous; **diesel particulate matter** (DPM) is a real concern for people living in cities or near to bus and lorry depots. Private cars have filters to remove DPMs and fewer are produced if there is plenty of oxygen for combustion (as in turbocharged engines).

Dealing with air pollution

Although humans can cause damage to the environment, they are also the only ones who are able to work out the best way of reducing this damage. Because scientists understand what a greenhouse gas does and why rain becomes acid, they can suggest ways to deal with these problems. For example, the greenhouse effect can be lessened by:

- reducing the cutting down of forests for cattle ranches and rice fields (burning the forests produces more carbon dioxide and reduces the number of plants that can absorb carbon dioxide)
- planting more forests (plants absorb carbon dioxide for photosynthesis)
- reducing the burning of fossil fuels by trying to find alternative energy sources.

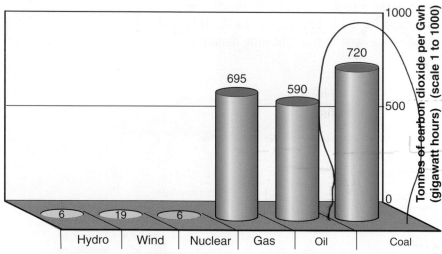

■ Carbon dioxide emission from various energy sources (2012)

All countries are being put under pressure to reduce their carbon emissions. In many countries rising energy demands are being met by coal, gas or oil power stations, which, as you can see from the graph, is not the way to reduce these greenhouse gases. Interestingly, nuclear power stations emit hardly any carbon dioxide, so countries with a substantial nuclear power programme have managed to reduce these emissions significantly. For example, France (80% nuclear) has, since 1970, halved its emissions of carbon; Japan (32% nuclear) has achieved a reduction of 20% (although the emissions have temporarily risen since the Fukushima nuclear power stations have been out of commission following the 2011 tsunami, and more oil and gas have therefore been imported and burned).

Acid rain can be reduced by:

- not burning coal, which has a high sulfur level
- building more efficient power stations that can clean the gases they let out into the atmosphere
- fitting cars with catalytic converters (these get rid of acid gases from the exhaust fumes).

Farmers sometimes add crushed chalk to their fields or lakes to neutralise the acid rain, but this is very expensive and takes a lot of time.

Exercise 7.5: Air pollution

1 Which one of these is not a fossil fuel: natural gas, wood, oil, coal?

2 Why do we say that carbon dioxide is a greenhouse gas?

Extension questions

Working Scientifically

3 Two students decided to investigate the effect of sulfur dioxide on the germination of oat seeds.
Twenty-five sets of apparatus were set up; five sets of apparatus for each of five different concentrations of sodium disulfite solution. (Sodium disulfite breaks down to release sulfur dioxide into the atmosphere.)
Fifty seeds were planted in each set of apparatus.

The table shows the results obtained one week after setting up the experiment.

Concentration of sodium disulfite/%	Number of seeds germinated in each set of apparatus	Mean number of seeds germinated out of 50 planted	Mean percentage germination
0.00	19, 19, 17, 20, 18		
0.05	18, 19, 18, 19, 19		
0.10	12, 13, 14, 11, 12		
0.50	0, 1, 0, 0, 1		
2.50	0, 0, 0, 0, 0		

(a) Copy the table. Calculate the mean number of seeds that germinated for each concentration, total number of seeds that germinated out of the 250 that were planted at each concentration. Use your results to complete the third column of the table.

(b) Using your mean values, calculate the mean percentage germination of seeds at each concentration. Use your results to complete the final column of the table.

(c) Plot the mean percentage germination results in the form of a bar chart.

(d) Why was the experiment repeated five times at each concentration?

(e) Water (i.e. 0% sodium disulfite solution) is used as a control. What is the purpose of this control?

(f) What is the lowest concentration of sodium disulfite that had a harmful effect on seed germination?

(g) How could the students modify the experiment to find a more accurate value for the concentration of sodium disulfite that had a harmful effect on seed germination?

(h) For this experiment, what are the independent (input) variables and the dependent (outcome) variables? Suggest two factors that might affect seed germination and that are controlled variables in this experiment.

(i) The sodium disulfite in the experiment released sulfur dioxide into the atmosphere in the apparatus.
   (i) Which human activity releases large amounts of sulfur dioxide into the natural environment?
   (ii) Suggest two other effects, apart from reducing seed germination, of sulfur dioxide on living organisms.

4 The following table contains information about the sources and effects of greenhouse gases.

Gas	Sources of gas	Percentage overall contribution to the greenhouse effect
Carbon dioxide	Burning forests, burning fossil fuels, production of cement	54
Chlorofluorocarbons (CFCs)	Aerosol propellants, refrigerants, coolants in air conditioners	21
Methane	Waste gases from domestic animals, rotting vegetation, rice growing	14
Nitrogen oxides	Exhaust gases from internal combustion engines, breakdown of fertilisers	7
Low-level ozone	Combination of nitrogen oxides with oxygen	2

(a) Present these results in the form of a bar chart.

(b) The only other greenhouse gas is water. Use the above data to calculate the greenhouse effect of water.

(c) Which of the gases shown in the table is produced by biological processes?

(d) What, exactly, is a greenhouse gas?

(e) Suggest three possibly harmful effects of greenhouse gases.

(f) Use the data in the table to suggest why the following are valuable conservation measures:
   (i) reducing forest clearances for cattle ranches
   (ii) improved insulation for houses
   (iii) the use of alternative energy sources, such as nuclear, windmills and wave machines.

(g) In 1900 the concentration of carbon dioxide in the atmosphere was 0.03%. In 1990 this had risen to 0.035%, and is expected to rise further to 0.055% by 2030.

   (i) By how much did the carbon dioxide concentration increase between 1900 and 1990?

   (ii) What is the expected increase in carbon dioxide concentration between 1990 and 2030?

   (iii) Suggest why the figure you calculated in (ii) is so much higher than your answer to (i).

Chemical reactions can be reversed

The different substances in a mixture can usually be separated quite easily (see Chapter 5). The methods used for these separations involve physical changes because the substances in the mixture have not been changed into different substances. It is more difficult to break up a compound formed by a chemical reaction into its elements but it is sometimes possible.

We know that chemical reactions are normally non-reversible, but in special circumstances some chemical reactions are in fact reversible. Another chemical reaction is needed to reverse a chemical reaction.

Decomposition

The type of chemical reaction that can break up a compound is called a **decomposition** reaction and usually requires a great deal of energy. The energy needed to break up some compounds can be supplied by thermal energy, in a type of reaction called a **thermal decomposition**. Other compounds can be broken up using electricity in a type of chemical reaction called **electrical decomposition** or **electrolysis**. To break up a compound by electrolysis, the compound needs to be molten or dissolved.

Some compounds are not very strongly bonded together and can be broken down into simpler materials by heat. The thermal decomposition of hydrated copper sulfate, for example, is reversible and forms a test for water.

Some examples of decomposition reactions are shown in the diagrams on the next pages.

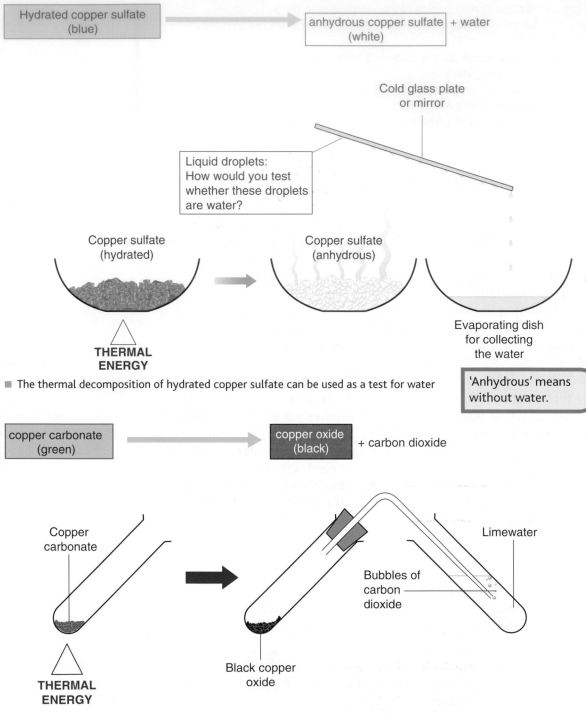

Hydrated copper sulfate (blue) → anhydrous copper sulfate (white) + water

Cold glass plate or mirror

Liquid droplets: How would you test whether these droplets are water?

Copper sulfate (hydrated)

Copper sulfate (anhydrous)

Evaporating dish for collecting the water

THERMAL ENERGY

■ The thermal decomposition of hydrated copper sulfate can be used as a test for water

'Anhydrous' means without water.

copper carbonate (green) → copper oxide (black) + carbon dioxide

Copper carbonate

Limewater

Bubbles of carbon dioxide

Black copper oxide

THERMAL ENERGY

■ The thermal decomposition of copper carbonate forms copper oxide and carbon dioxide

| potassium permanganate (VII) (purple) | $\longrightarrow$ | potassium manganate(III) + oxygen + | manganese dioxide (black) |

Oxygen gas: How could you collect and test for this gas?

potassium permanganate(VII)

potassium manganate(III) + manganese dioxide

■ The thermal decomposition of potassium permanganate(VII) forms three new products

The thermal decomposition of calcium carbonate in limestone can be represented by the following word equation:

calcium carbonate (white) $\rightarrow$ calcium oxide + carbon dioxide

The calcium carbonate must be heated very strongly for this final reaction to happen. The heating can take place on a large scale, where crushed limestone is heated inside a special type of oven called a kiln. These lime kilns can still be seen in many parts of the country where limestone is common. Calcium oxide is called **lime** and is an important product for agriculture. Chemists dissolve lime in water to produce slaked lime (calcium hydroxide) and then use this slaked lime to neutralise acidic soils.

Go further

Cobalt chloride, $CoCl_2$, forms a crystal structure that can be rearranged in the presence of water.

As the humidity increases, and water is absorbed by $CoCl_2$, the crystal structure firstly allows two water molecules to surround each cobalt atom, forming the **dihydrate**, ('two water molecules'). Cobalt chloride dihydrate is purple. The **hydration** reaction may be represented by the following chemical reaction:

$CoCl_2 + 2H_2O$ (blue) $\rightarrow$ $CoCl_2 \cdot 2H_2O$ (purple)

As the humidity increases further, four more water molecules can surround each cobalt atom, forming the **hexahydrate** ('six water molecules'):

$$CoCl_2 \cdot 2H_2O + 4H_2O \rightarrow CoCl_2 \cdot 6H_2O$$
(purple)   (pink)

Heating the hydrated forms of cobalt chloride reverses the reactions above, returning cobalt chloride to the blue, water-free, or **anhydrous**, state.

- This is **not** a typical decomposition reaction, because it is reversible.
- Water is 'freed' in these reactions, which are known as **dehydration reactions**.
- The heating can be very gentle, no more than the thermal energy provided by standing the cobalt chloride on a radiator.

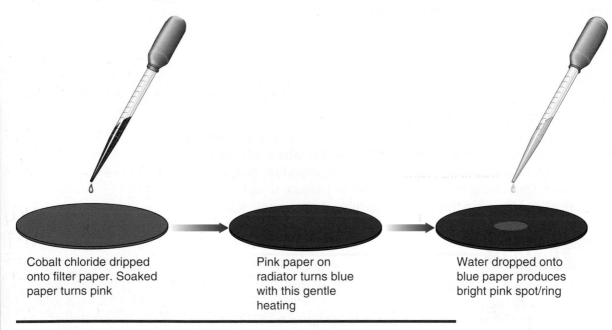

Cobalt chloride dripped onto filter paper. Soaked paper turns pink

Pink paper on radiator turns blue with this gentle heating

Water dropped onto blue paper produces bright pink spot/ring

Investigation: Mass change on heating

The aim of this experiment is to investigate the effect of heating on the mass of substances.

Empty crucible

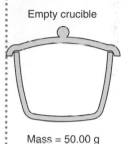

Mass = 50.00 g

Crucible and copper carbonate

Mass = 51.24 g

Crucible and copper oxide

Mass = 50.80 g

Two students heated some copper carbonate in a crucible. They recorded the mass of the crucible and contents before and after heating.

The word equation for this reaction is:

copper carbonate → copper oxide + carbon dioxide

1   What mass of carbon dioxide is given off in this reaction?

The students then heated some magnesium in another crucible. They worked carefully and did not lose any of the magnesium oxide that formed. They recorded the mass of the crucible and contents before and after heating.

- Mass of empty crucible: 50.00 g
- Mass of crucible and magnesium: 50.12 g
- Mass of crucible and magnesium oxide: 50.26 g

2   Why does the mass of the contents of the crucible increase in this reaction?

3   State the principle of conservation of mass.

Exercise 7.6: Reversed reactions

1   Do you think there will be any change in mass in the thermal decomposition of copper sulfate? Explain your answer.

2   During the thermal decomposition of copper carbonate, carbon dioxide is released. What would be the positive result of a test for this gas?

3   Calcium oxide is produced by the thermal decomposition of calcium carbonate. Explain why calcium oxide is an important agricultural product. *Hint:* You will need to research 'slaked lime' use in farming.

8 The reactions of metals

You have seen in previous chapters that new substances can be formed during chemical reactions. A new substance formed by combining two or more different elements is called a **compound**. During a combustion reaction, oxygen from the air can combine with another element to form a compound called an **oxide**.

If an element takes part in a chemical reaction easily, we say that it is **reactive**. Some **metals** are very **unreactive**; gold and silver, for example, do not take part in many chemical reactions. Most metals are reactive and some are very reactive indeed. We can arrange all the metals into a sort of 'league table' of reactivity, depending on how easily they react with other substances. This ordered list of reactivity is called the **reactivity series**. It can be worked out by comparing the reaction of different metals with oxygen, water and acids.

Metals and oxygen

You should already have an idea of how metals react with oxygen (see Chapter 2) and we also know that some metals react much more quickly than others do. Reactions with oxygen are called **oxidations**. Products of oxidation reactions are called oxides. The word equation for one of these oxidation reactions is shown:

metal + oxygen → metal oxide

The different metals can be compared in their reaction with oxygen using the apparatus shown in the diagram on next page.

Like many chemical reactions, this reaction will not begin until some thermal energy is supplied. Overall, combustion is **exothermic**, meaning it gives out more thermal energy than it takes in.

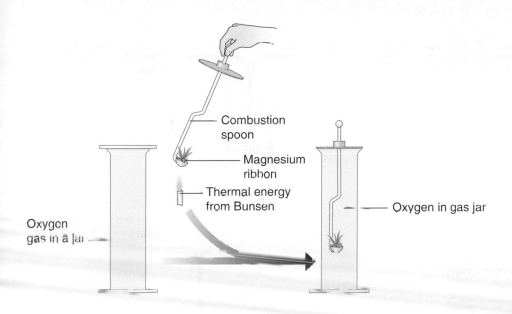

This table lists the results obtained in a series of experiments.

■ The reactions of some common metals with oxygen

Metal	Reaction with oxygen	Product
Sodium	Burns very quickly even after gentle heating	Sodium peroxide (a pale yellow powder)
Calcium	Burns easily with gentle heating	Calcium oxide (white powder)
Magnesium	Burns easily with a brilliant white flame	Magnesium oxide (grey-white powder)
Iron	Burns slowly and only if there is strong heating and the iron is powdered or in strands	Iron oxide (black powder)
Copper	Does not burn, but a black layer is formed on the surface of the metal	Copper oxide (black powder)
Gold	No reaction, even with strong heating	

SAFETY! Sodium burns so violently that it is dangerous. You would not be allowed to burn sodium in the school laboratory!

Comparing oxides of metals and non-metals

As we saw in Chapter 2, you can tell the difference between metals and non-metals because they have many different physical properties. They also have some different chemical properties. When a (reactive) metal reacts with oxygen, the oxide formed in the reaction will be a **base**. In contrast, when a non-metal reacts with oxygen to form an oxide, it will be an **acid**. The diagram on the next page shows how oxides can be tested to see if they are acidic or basic.

You will find out more about acids and bases (**alkalis**) in Chapter 9.

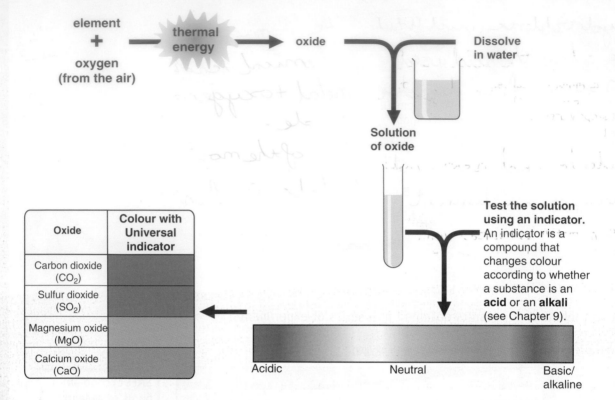

Oxide	Colour with Universal indicator
Carbon dioxide (CO_2)	
Sulfur dioxide (SO_2)	
Magnesium oxide (MgO)	
Calcium oxide (CaO)	

Test the solution using an indicator. An indicator is a compound that changes colour according to whether a substance is an **acid** or an **alkali** (see Chapter 9).

Acidic   Neutral   Basic/alkaline

Metals and water

If a **reactive metal** (in other words, a metal high in the reactivity series), for example sodium or calcium, is placed in water, it reacts vigorously to form the **hydroxide**. For example:

water + sodium → sodium hydroxide + hydrogen

This reaction is strongly exothermic and the thermal energy ignites the hydrogen. The reaction of potassium with water is even more exciting!

Less reactive metals react with **steam** to form the oxide and hydrogen:

water + metal → metal oxide + hydrogen

This occurs with magnesium, iron, aluminium and zinc.

water + magnesium → magnesium oxide + hydrogen

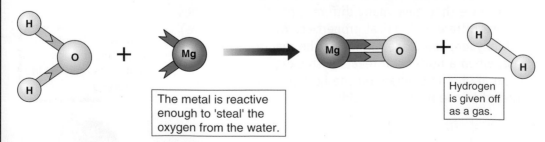

The metal is reactive enough to 'steal' the oxygen from the water.

Hydrogen is given off as a gas.

> **Rule:**
>
> Metal oxides are basic.
>
> Non-metal oxides are acidic.

Did you know?

It is very hard to make aluminium react with water, because it has already reacted with oxygen! Aluminium metal very quickly gets covered with a thin layer of aluminium oxide. This layer stops water molecules reaching the metal, so they cannot react with it. As a result, we can use aluminium for very lightweight pans and kettles without worrying about any reaction with water.

Some metals do not react with water at all. Imagine what would happen if a copper pan reacted with water or if gold reacted with water and you forgot to remove a gold ring when you washed your hands! Some metals react quite slowly with water (magnesium is an example), but some react so violently that they must be kept under a layer of oil or they would react with the water vapour in the air.

The following table lists the results of experiments in which metals and water are allowed to react together.

■ The reactions of some common metals with water

Metal	Reaction with water	Products
Sodium	Reacts very violently and catches fire	Hydrogen gas + sodium hydroxide solution
Calcium	Reacts quite quickly	Hydrogen gas + calcium hydroxide in solution
Magnesium	Reacts slowly with water but quite vigorously with steam	Hydrogen gas + solid magnesium oxide
Iron	No reaction in cold water*, but iron will react with steam	Hydrogen gas + solid iron oxide
Copper	No reaction	
Gold	No reaction	

*This is true in principle but in practice iron will rust in cold water, unless the water has had all the dissolved oxygen taken out.

Metals and acids

Acids are compounds and include hydrogen in their structure. You will learn more about acids in Chapter 9. When a metal reacts with an acid, the metal replaces the hydrogen in the compound and the hydrogen is given off as a gas. As well as hydrogen, another product, called a **salt**, is produced.

Most metals react with acids. For example, if magnesium is put into hydrochloric acid, this reaction takes place:

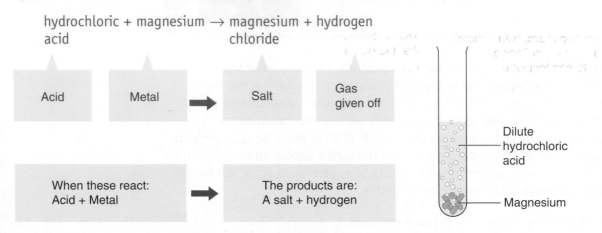

hydrochloric + magnesium → magnesium + hydrogen
acid   chloride

| Acid | Metal | → | Salt | Gas given off |

| When these react: Acid + Metal | → | The products are: A salt + hydrogen |

Dilute hydrochloric acid

Magnesium

The following diagram shows what is happening in the reaction of magnesium with hydrochloric acid.

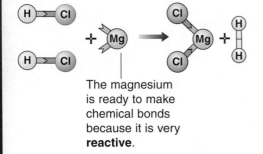

The magnesium is ready to make chemical bonds because it is very **reactive**.

The magnesium (Mg) has **displaced** the hydrogen (H) ('displaced' means 'has taken the place of', see later in this chapter). The presence of hydrogen can be tested using a lighted splint.

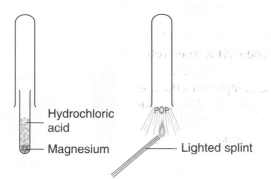

Hydrochloric acid

Magnesium

POP

Lighted splint

| An acid reacts with a metal, and gas is collected in an upturned test tube. | This test shows that the gas is hydrogen. |

■ The test for hydrogen gas

If we are going to compare the reactivity of metals with acids, we should always use the same acid in the tests. This table gives results for the reaction of some different metals with dilute hydrochloric acid.

■ The reactions of some common metals with hydrochloric acid

Metal	Reaction with dilute hydrochloric acid	Products
Magnesium	Reacts very quickly	Hydrogen gas + magnesium chloride in solution
Zinc	Reacts slowly	Hydrogen gas + zinc chloride in solution
Iron	Reacts slowly, unless the mixture is warmed	Hydrogen gas + iron chloride in solution
Copper	No reaction	
Gold	No reaction	

This next table gives results for the reaction of some different metals with sulfuric acid.

■ The reactions of some common metals with sulfuric acid

Metal	Reaction with dilute sulfuric acid	Products
Magnesium	Reacts very quickly	Hydrogen gas + magnesium sulfate in solution
Zinc	Reacts slowly	Hydrogen gas + zinc sulfate in solution
Iron	Reacts slowly, unless the mixture is warmed	Hydrogen gas + iron sulfate in solution
Copper	No reaction	
Gold	No reaction	

The reactivity series

If you look back at these tables of results, you should be able to see that we can arrange the metals in a list according to how reactive they are. As you have learned, this list is called the **reactivity series** and a short version is shown in the diagram on the right.

The reactivity series gives a league table of metals, according to how easily they react with other substances.

Hydrogen and carbon are **not metals**, but they are often placed in the reactivity series. These elements play an important part in some reactions with metals, so it is useful to know where they fit.

Most reactive

Potassium (K)
Sodium (Na)
Calcium (Ca)
Magnesium (Mg)
Aluminium (Al)
Zinc (Zn)
Carbon (C)
Iron (Fe)
Lead (Pb)
Hydrogen (H)
Copper (Cu)
Silver (Ag)
Least reactive Gold (Au)

Competition between metals: displacement reactions

Metals that are high in the reactivity series are more likely to react than metals that are low in the series. If two metals are present in the same solution, the more reactive metal will bind onto any other chemical in the solution. For example, a chemical reaction occurs when a piece of zinc is placed in a solution of blue copper sulfate. The zinc turns darker and the blue copper sulfate turns paler. If this sounds complicated, have a look at the following diagram; it should help you to understand the process.

zinc + copper sulfate → zinc sulfate + copper

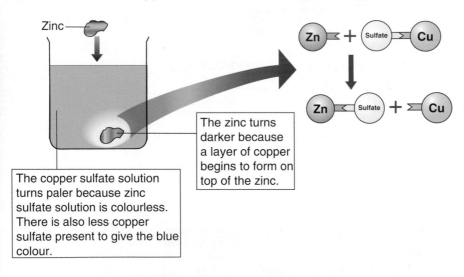

The zinc turns darker because a layer of copper begins to form on top of the zinc.

The copper sulfate solution turns paler because zinc sulfate solution is colourless. There is also less copper sulfate present to give the blue colour.

The zinc and copper compete for the sulfate. Zinc is more reactive, which means it can form stronger bonds, so it displaces the copper from the copper sulfate.

The kind of reaction in which one metal replaces another is called a **displacement reaction**. The metals displace one another in a regular order and we can predict this order from the reactivity series. The predictions can be checked by carrying out a series of experiments; in these experiments different metals are added to different solutions of metal salts.

The results of one set of experiments are shown in the following table.

Metal	Reaction with magnesium chloride solution	Reaction with iron nitrate solution	Reaction with lead chloride solution	Reaction with copper sulfate solution	Reaction with silver nitrate solution
Magnesium	✘	✔	✔	✔	✔
Zinc	✘	✔	✔	✔	✔
Iron	✘	✘	✔	✔	✔
Lead	✘	✘	✘	✔	✔
Copper	✘	✘	✘	✘	✔
Silver	✘	✘	✘	✘	✘

In this table, a ✔ sign means that a displacement reaction took place and a ✘ sign means that no displacement reaction took place.

These results show a pattern that confirms the order of metals in the reactivity series. A displacement reaction only takes place when the metal being added is higher in the reactivity series than the metal that is already present (in the salt solution).

For example, iron **can** displace lead from a lead chloride solution because iron is higher in the series (i.e. more reactive) than lead.

iron + lead chloride → iron chloride + lead

However, iron **cannot** displace magnesium from magnesium chloride solution because iron is lower in the series than magnesium.

We can use displacement reactions to make new salts from salts we already have. If we need some magnesium sulfate and we have some copper sulfate and some magnesium, we can make magnesium sulfate by mixing the two chemicals in water. The magnesium will displace the copper and magnesium sulfate will be formed.

magnesium + copper sulfate → magnesium sulfate + copper

Displacement from solids: metals and metal oxides

Not all displacement reactions involve solid metals and metal salt solutions. Displacement reactions can also take place between solid metals and solid metal oxides. However, these reactions can be quite dangerous and are not so easy to carry out in a school laboratory.

One example that can be demonstrated in a school laboratory involves the reaction of powdered iron and copper oxide.

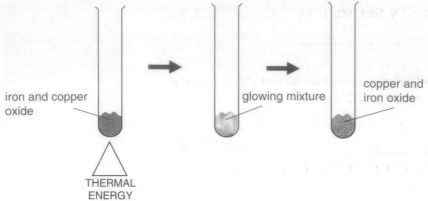

iron and copper oxide

glowing mixture

copper and iron oxide

THERMAL ENERGY

■ Displacing a metal from a metal oxide

THINK ABOUT IT!

Give two ways in which you know that a chemical reaction has taken place.

The **iron** has **gained oxygen**. We can say that:

● the iron has been **oxidised**
● it is an **oxidation** reaction.

The **copper oxide** has **lost** the **oxygen** to the **iron**. We can say that:

● the copper oxide has been **reduced**
● this is called a **reduction** reaction.

We can also say that:

● iron is a reducing agent
● copper oxide is an oxidising agent for iron.

In this reaction the iron and copper are competing for the oxygen but because iron is more reactive (higher up the reactivity series) than copper, it steals the oxygen away from the copper oxide.

Another well-known example of this kind of reaction occurs when powdered aluminium and iron oxide are heated together.

aluminium + iron oxide → iron + aluminium oxide

Once this reaction is started, it carries on very quickly and gives out enough thermal (internal) energy to keep the iron molten. The reaction is called the **thermite reaction**. This thermite reaction is very useful in industry when a small amount of molten iron at a high temperature is needed. This reaction is used to join two lengths of railway line together. So much thermal (internal) energy is given out that it melts the ends of the rails and they form a very strong joint as they cool together.

8 *The reactions of metals*

Using the reactivity series to predict chemical reactions

From the reactions we have learned about in the last few sections, we can make a useful summary that will allow you to use the reactivity series to predict the outcome of chemical reactions.

● The reactivity series allows us to predict **what** will happen.

For example, it tells us that sodium is a very reactive metal. If sodium is added to water, we know that there will be a violent reaction and hydrogen gas will be given off.

● The reactivity series can also let us predict **how fast** a reaction will occur.

For example, calcium fizzes gently when it is placed in water because bubbles of hydrogen gas are given off. Some thermal (internal) energy is given off and the water becomes warm. Potassium is higher in the reactivity series, so we would predict that it would react more violently with water than calcium does. In fact potassium reacts so violently that it whizzes around in the water, the hydrogen bursts into flames and the water can get very hot! Potassium and hydrogen are **a long way apart** in the reactivity series, which is why the reaction to 'steal' the oxygen from the hydrogen in the water is so violent.

■ Potassium reacts violently with water

If two metals are **close together** in the series, then the reaction between them will be **slow and gentle**. For example, when powdered lead and copper oxide are heated together, copper is displaced from the copper oxide and lead oxide is produced, but because the two metals have almost the same reactivity, the reaction goes on very slowly.

● The reactivity series can also predict **how stable** a compound is likely to be.

Metals that are high in the reactivity series form compounds so quickly because they can bond very tightly to other elements. Once one of these compounds has been formed, it is very difficult to break them down again – scientists say they are hard to **decompose**. For example, copper carbonate is easily decomposed by heating but potassium carbonate will not decompose, even if it is heated strongly for a long time.

copper carbonate → copper oxide + carbon dioxide
thermal energy

potassium carbonate → no reaction
thermal energy

Rules for predicting chemical changes

- Reactions of metals are faster and stronger the nearer the metal is to the top of the reactivity series.
- Metals higher up the series can displace metals lower down the series from their compounds.
- Compounds of metals higher up in the series are more stable than the compounds of metals lower down in the series.

Here is a summary that you can use to predict what will happen in chemical reactions:

Predicting chemical reactions with the reactivity series

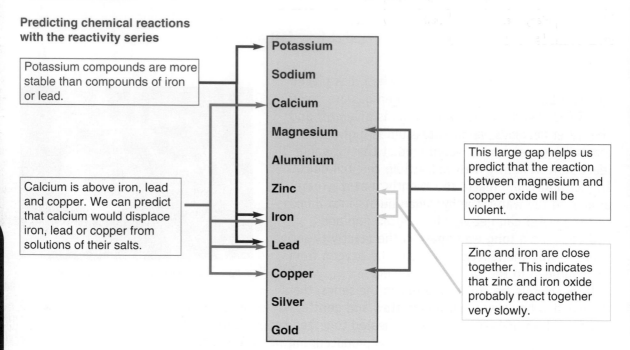

Potassium compounds are more stable than compounds of iron or lead.

Calcium is above iron, lead and copper. We can predict that calcium would displace iron, lead or copper from solutions of their salts.

Potassium
Sodium
Calcium
Magnesium
Aluminium
Zinc
Iron
Lead
Copper
Silver
Gold

This large gap helps us predict that the reaction between magnesium and copper oxide will be violent.

Zinc and iron are close together. This indicates that zinc and iron oxide probably react together very slowly.

Using the reactivity series: understanding the uses of metals

Metals are used in many industries and activities. Scientists who understand the reactivity series can suggest which metal is most likely to be useful for a particular job. There are usually several things to think about when making a choice of a metal to use:

- Is it cheap enough?
- Is it unreactive, so that it will not combine with other substances and change its properties?
- Can it be made into useful shapes easily?

■ Some ways in which the reactivity series can predict how metals may most usefully be used

Metal	Use	How reactivity suits its purpose
Silver	Electrical contacts	Very unreactive, so it does not corrode inside electrical equipment
Gold	Jewellery Spectacle frames	Very unreactive, so it does not corrode when in contact with skin
Lead	Roofing	Does not react with water, so is ideal as a waterproof roof; soft enough to be shaped easily
Copper	Piping Electrical wiring	Does not react with fluids moving through pipes and does not corrode
Iron	Many uses in engineering	Quite reactive, but it can be protected from corrosion

Exercise 8.1: The reactivity series

1 A piece of zinc is placed in silver nitrate solution. As the zinc dissolves, the solution turns grey and a silver coating appears on the zinc.
   (a) Which is more reactive, zinc or silver?
   (b) Copy and complete the following word equation:

   zinc + silver nitrate $\rightarrow$ _____

2 Look at the following situations. For each one, say whether a reaction will take place. Give a reason for each of your answers.
   (a) Iron heated with copper oxide
   (b) Magnesium placed in dilute hydrochloric acid
   (c) Copper placed in dilute sulfuric acid
   (d) Magnesium placed in copper sulfate solution
   (e) Silver warmed with water

Extension question

Working Scientifically

3 You have been given some pieces of an unknown metal, called M. You also have solutions of copper sulfate, zinc sulfate, iron sulfate and magnesium sulfate.
   Metal M is thought to be either copper, magnesium or zinc.

   (a) How could you test to see what metal M is?
   (b) Metal M reacts with hydrochloric acid and gives out a gas. Describe a useful test you could carry out on the gas and suggest what the result would be.
   (c) Metal M can be converted to a carbonate. The carbonate decomposes if it is heated and a gas is given off. What is this gas? How could you test for its identity?

Corrosion of metals

As we have seen, metals can react with oxygen to form oxides. Metals high in the reactivity series react more quickly with oxygen than metals lower in the reactivity series.

Most metals turn dull when they are exposed to the air. The dullness is usually a coating of metal oxide, formed when the metal reacts with oxygen in the air. For example:

aluminium + oxygen → aluminium oxide

This layer can be useful because it stops the oxygen getting at the metal under the coating. The layer is so useful that sometimes it is deliberately made thicker if it is especially important that the metal does not corrode (see later in this chapter).

Copper reacts with carbon dioxide and oxygen in the atmosphere and forms a thin coat of a green compound called **verdigris**. This can often be seen where copper has been used to make a roof on a building.

Corrosion is generally a slow process, although very reactive metals, such as sodium and potassium, are kept in a bottle of oil so that they can't react with oxygen in the air. The metals at the bottom of the reactivity series hardly corrode at all, which is one reason why silver and gold are so important in the production of jewellery.

■ This copper roof has been coated in green verdigris where the copper has reacted with oxygen from the air

Rusting is the corrosion of iron

Of all the metals that can be obtained from the Earth, iron is used more than any other. There are a number of reasons for this.

- Iron is easy to obtain because there is a lot of iron ore in the Earth's crust.
- The process of separating iron from its ore is quite an easy one. Iron ores are refined in a blast furnace. The product of the blast furnace is called pig iron and contains about 4% carbon. Cast iron is made when pig iron is melted again in furnaces (see later in this chapter). This cast iron contains between 2% and 6% carbon.
- Iron can be mixed with other substances to make its properties suitable for a wide range of jobs. Most iron is used in this way to make **steel**. (Steel contains less carbon than pig iron and doesn't shatter or crack so easily.)

Rusting is the name given to the corrosion of iron and steel. This process is a problem because so many structures made by humans get their strength from iron or steel. It is important that we understand the processes involved in rusting, so that we can do something to stop them.

Investigation: The rusting of iron

Iron nails are a very convenient source of iron for this experiment. It is easy to get a set of nails that are all the same size and shape, so that the experiment will give reliable results. The following diagram shows an experiment to investigate the conditions that cause rusting.

No water	No air	Air and water (control)	Air and warm water	Air, water and salt	Air, water and acid
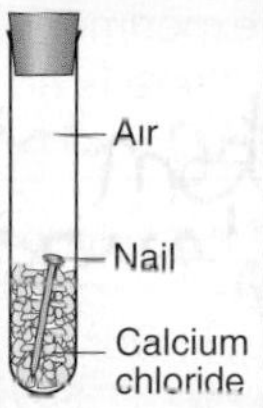 Air — Nail — Calcium chloride	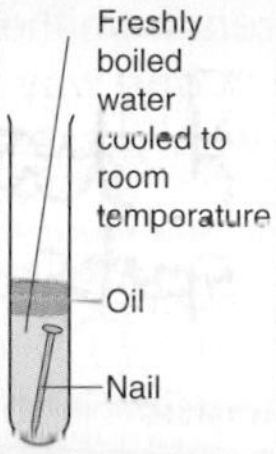 Freshly boiled water cooled to room temperature — Oil — Nail	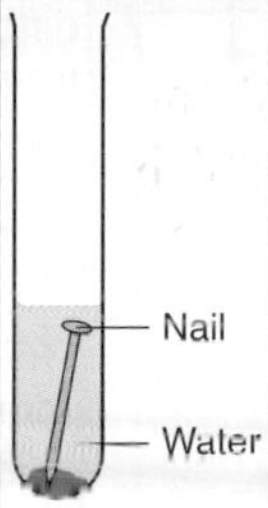 Nail — Water	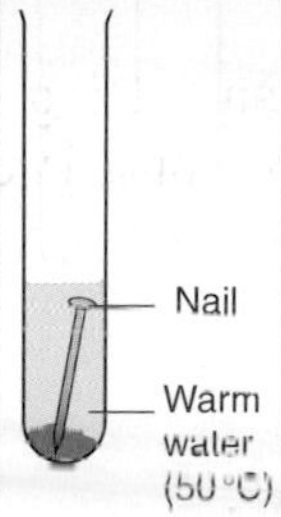 Nail — Warm water (50 °C)	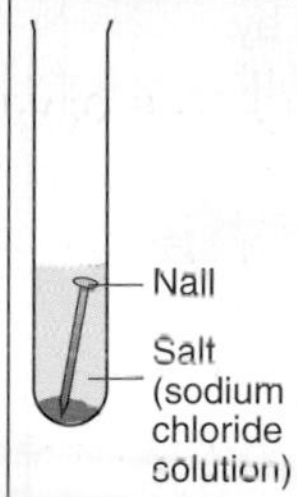 Nail — Salt (sodium chloride solution)	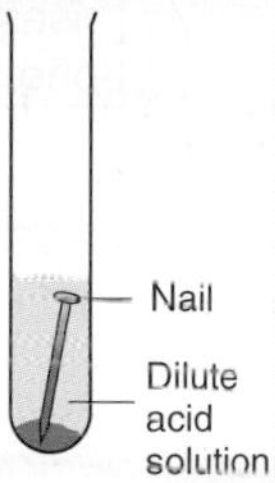 Nail — Dilute acid solution
Special conditions The calcium chloride removes **water** from the air. The rubber bung means that no more water vapour can enter.	**Special conditions** Boiling removes the air from the water. A layer of oil means no more air can enter the water.	**Special conditions** This tube is the one that all other results can be compared to. No rubber bung means that air can enter the tube.	**Special conditions** This only differs from the control tube by the temperature of the water.	**Special conditions** Make sure that the temperature is the same as the control tube.	
Results NO RUST	**Results** NO RUST	**Results** RUSTY	**Results** VERY RUSTY	**Results** VERY RUSTY	**Result** VERY RUSTY

1 What conclusions can be drawn from this experiment?

Rusting is the combination of oxygen with iron

The experiment that follows shows that iron combines with **oxygen** in the air when rusting takes place.

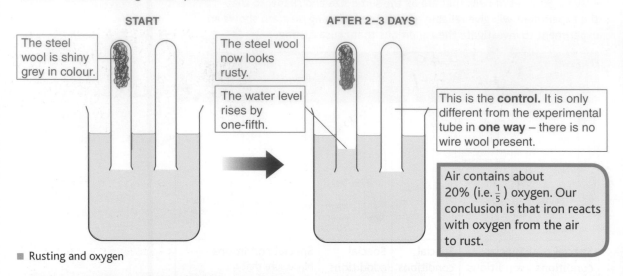

START   AFTER 2–3 DAYS

The steel wool is shiny grey in colour.

The steel wool now looks rusty.

The water level rises by one-fifth.

This is the **control.** It is only different from the experimental tube in **one way** – there is no wire wool present.

Air contains about 20% (i.e. $\frac{1}{5}$) oxygen. Our conclusion is that iron reacts with oxygen from the air to rust.

■ Rusting and oxygen

Look back at the investigation. Think about two ways in which you could speed up this experiment so that you would not have to wait for 2–3 days.

So we have seen that rusting is the combination of iron with oxygen. The material that we call 'rust', the brown flaky material that forms on iron and steel, is actually a special kind of oxide called **hydrated iron oxide**. The word equation for the formation of rust is:

iron + oxygen + water → hydrated iron oxide (rust)

Once we understand the conditions needed for rusting to occur, we can explain our observations about rusting in different conditions.

Rusting is a problem because the hydrated iron oxide is very brittle (breaks easily) and weak. Since so many objects made by humans get their strength from iron or steel, this weakening could be extremely dangerous. For example, many cars must be scrapped because the bodywork has rusted, even though the mechanical parts, such as the engine and gearbox, are still working quite well.

Understanding rusting

Crashed aircraft in the desert **do not rust** as there is almost no water in the desert air.

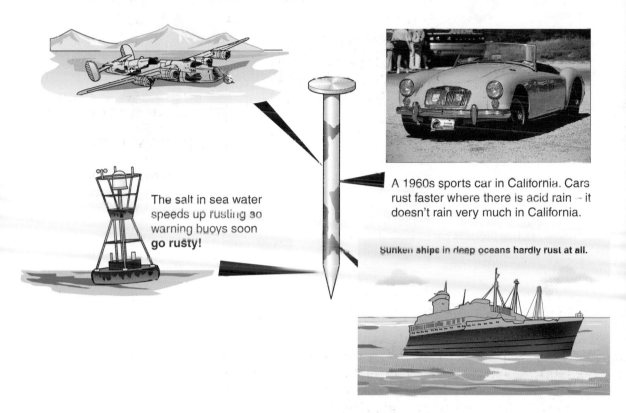

The salt in sea water speeds up rusting so warning buoys soon **go rusty!**

A 1960s sports car in California. Cars rust faster where there is acid rain – it doesn't rain very much in California.

Sunken ships in deep oceans hardly rust at all.

Prevention of corrosion

Because iron and steel are so important in industries such as building and engineering, they must be protected from corrosion. There are two ways in which iron and steel can be protected:

- by forming a **physical barrier** to keep out air or water
- by attaching the iron to a more reactive metal, such as magnesium or zinc, that can oxidise more easily than the iron does. This is known as **sacrificial protection.**

The diagrams on the next page describe these two methods.

Barrier methods keep air and water out

Oil or **grease** keep water away from moving parts of machinery, such as a bike chain.

'**Tin' cans** are about 99% steel (cheap) with a very thin covering of tin (very expensive).This protects the steel, especially from acid foods such as tinned fruits.

Painting a cover onto a steel bridge. Paint is cheap and a large area can be covered quickly.

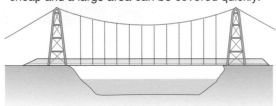

A plastic coating can be put on a chain-link fence.

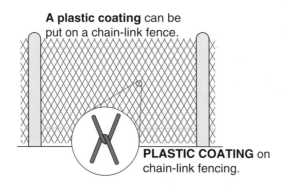

PLASTIC COATING on chain-link fencing.

Once rust starts to appear on metal, it must be rubbed away (usually with sandpaper) and then the base metal can be carefully repainted.

Sacrificial protection

Zinc panels on a ship's steel hull will oxidise first as zinc is more reactive than iron.

Magnesium is bolted to underground oil and gas pipes.

Zinc coating (galvanising) on steel buckets and screws combines a physical barrier with a sacrificial metal but the zinc is expensive and adds extra weight.

Electroplating uses electricity to put a thin layer of an attractive (but expensive) metal onto iron or steel. Chrome parts on a car or motorbike are steel with a very thin layer of chromium on top.

Each method has certain advantages and disadvantages.

- Physical barriers are often cheap and can be used to cover large areas of iron or steel. The main disadvantage is that once the coating is scratched or damaged, then air and water can get to the iron and rusting will begin. Physical barriers cannot be used if the iron is being rubbed or worn, such as when it is made up into railway lines.
- Sacrificial protection can be used to cover areas of iron or steel that are often bumped or rubbed during normal use. The method is usually more expensive than coating and the more reactive metal will eventually be used up.

Galvanising involves both types of protection

Iron and steel can be protected by coating them in a thin layer of zinc. This is usually done by dipping the metal object in a big bath of molten zinc. Thirty per cent of all the zinc extracted from the Earth is used for this process, which is known as galvanising. Galvanising is used:

- for car panels, especially in more expensive cars
- for motorway crash barriers
- for dustbins
- for iron roofing sheets
- for girders used to support parts of buildings.

The zinc acts as a barrier against corrosion by keeping out air and water. The advantage of this type of coating is that if it is scratched, the iron is still protected, as zinc is a more reactive metal.

Exercise 8.2: Corrosion

1 Copy and complete these paragraphs:
   (a) Corrosion involves a reaction between a _____ and some substance in the _____. In most cases an _____ is formed on the surface of the metal.
   (b) Rusting is the corrosion of _____ and _____. This is a dangerous process because the _____ is weak and brittle. Rusting can be prevented by coating the metal with, for example, _____. Another method of prevention involves 'sacrificing' a second metal, such as _____.

2 The rusting of car bodies is the main reason why cars need to be scrapped.
   (a) Write a word equation for the rusting of iron.
   (b) Why do cars rust more quickly in the UK than in California?
   (c) Give two ways in which car manufacturers can protect cars against rust.

3 Galvanising is a method used to stop corrosion.
   (a) Why is galvanising such an effective method of protection?
   (b) Give three examples of the use of galvanising.
   (c) Why can't coating be used for preventing corrosion of railway lines?

4 A scientist was trying to work out the conditions needed for rusting. She set up five test tubes as shown in the diagram.

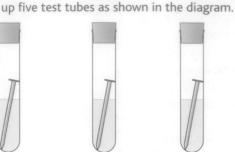

Layer of oil

1. Water + air	2. Salty water + air	3. Warm water + air	4. Warm salty water + air	4. Warm, boiled salty water

After ten days she took the nails out of the tubes and measured how much of each nail was covered in rust. She wrote down the results in a table, giving a figure of '0' if there was no rust and '1' if the nail was completely covered in rust.

Tube number	Amount of rust
1	0.4
2	0.6
3	0.7
4	1.0
5	

(a) Which had the bigger effect on rusting, salt or warmth? Give a reason for your answer.

(b) She did not write in the result for the fifth tube. What do you think the result would be? Give a reason for your answer.

(c) Draw a bar chart of these results.

Extension questions

5 Look back to Question 3. Design a fair test using galvanised nails to investigate whether galvanising offers double protection for steel.

6 Use the internet or your library to find out about stainless steel – how is it different from iron and how is it made?

8   The reactions of metals

7 Andrew carried out an experiment to investigate how much change in thermal (internal) energy went on when magnesium reacted with a copper sulfate solution. During the reaction the magnesium displaced the copper, and the copper was left at the bottom of the tube.

He mixed different amounts of magnesium powder with copper sulfate solution in a set of boiling tubes. He carefully measured the temperature of the copper sulfate solution before he added the magnesium powder. The temperature was measured again when the reaction was completed. His results are shown in the table.

Mass of magnesium/g	Starting temperature/°C	Final temperature/°C	Rise in temperature/°C
0.00	22	22	
0.25	23	30	
0.50	23	38	
0.75	22	46	
1.00	22	55	
1.25	22	61	
1.50	23	68	
1.75	24	69	
2.00	23	68	
2.25	22	67	
2.50	23	68	

(a) Complete the fourth column of the table to show the **rise** in temperature.
(b) Write down a word equation for this reaction.
(c) What is the independent (input) variable for this reaction?
(d) What is the dependent (outcome) variable in this experiment?
(e) Is the reaction exothermic or endothermic?
(f) Using graph paper, plot a suitable graph of the results.
(g) Describe and explain the shape of the curve you have plotted.
(h) What steps would need to be taken to make sure that this was a fair test?
(i) 25 g of copper sulfate solution was used in each of the experiments. What was the total mass of the chemicals in the boiling tube at the end of the experiment when 1.50 g of magnesium was added? Explain your answer.

Extraction of metals from ores

As we have seen, metals have important properties that are useful to humans. Most metals are not found in a pure state in the environment but instead are found combined with other substances as **ores**.

The reactivity series can help us to predict how difficult it will be to separate a metal from other substances.

A few metals are so unreactive that they can be found uncombined (as the element) in the ground. Because they are found as pure metals in nature, they are called **native metals**. These metals include gold, platinum and silver.

Most metals are found combined with other substances in **compounds** – usually the compound contains the metal and either oxygen or sulfur. An ore is a rock or mineral that contains a metal. The rock will need to be broken down if we are to obtain the metal. There are three main steps involved in the extraction of the metal:

● locating and mining the ore
● decomposing the ore to release the metal
● purifying the metal, so that its properties exactly suit its purpose.

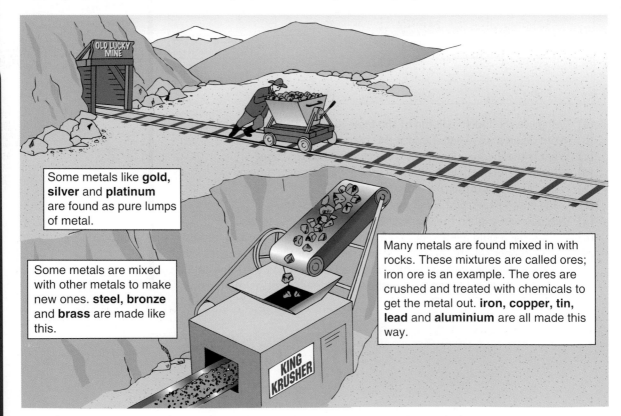

Some metals like **gold, silver** and **platinum** are found as pure lumps of metal.

Some metals are mixed with other metals to make new ones. **steel, bronze** and **brass** are made like this.

Many metals are found mixed in with rocks. These mixtures are called ores; iron ore is an example. The ores are crushed and treated with chemicals to get the metal out. **iron, copper, tin, lead** and **aluminium** are all made this way.

■ Extracting metals found underground

To decide whether it is worth mining an ore, the following points are considered:

- how much ore there is
- whether the mining will be dangerous
- how expensive the extraction and purification will be
- whether the metal has important uses
- whether the mining and extraction will damage the environment.

Methods of extraction

The extraction of metals from their ores involves chemical reactions to break down the compounds and release the metal. These chemical reactions are examples of **decomposition**, because the compound is decomposed (broken down). The reactions are also **reduction** reactions because the reactions reduce the number of elements combined with the metal. Many ores are oxides, so reduction in this case means the amount of oxygen combined with the metal is reduced.

There are three main methods that can be used to reduce ores and extract metals:

- **roasting** the ore (using only thermal energy)
- **displacing** the metal by heating with carbon
- using electrical energy to split the compound in a process called **electrolysis**.

Understanding the reactivity series means that scientists can predict which method will be needed. The higher up the reactivity series a metal is, the more stable its compounds will be. The very stable compounds will need a great deal of energy to reduce them to the pure metal. The following table lists some ores, the metals they contain and the method needed to extract the metal.

■ Methods of extraction of some common metal

Metal	Position in the reactivity series	Ore	Method of extraction
Aluminium	High – above carbon	Bauxite (mainly aluminium oxide)	Electrolysis
Iron	Middle – below carbon	Hematite (iron oxide)	Heating with carbon
Lead	Middle – below carbon	Galena (mainly lead sulfide)	Heating with carbon
Copper	Middle – below carbon	Malachite (mainly copper carbonate)	Heating with carbon
Mercury	Very low	Cinnabar (mainly mercury sulfide)	Heating in the air
Silver	Very low	Silver oxide (some silver is also found as 'native' silver)	Heating in the air

Thermal decomposition: extraction by thermal energy alone

Thermal energy can decompose some compounds of the very unreactive metals. For example, silver can be produced from silver oxide by strong heating in air, as shown in the diagram on the right.

Mercury, and sometimes copper (depending on the ore it is found in), can also be obtained in this way. This is a very inexpensive method, but it cannot be used for the compounds of the more reactive metals.

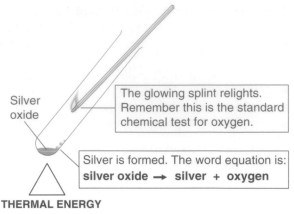

Silver oxide

The glowing splint relights. Remember this is the standard chemical test for oxygen.

Silver is formed. The word equation is:
silver oxide → silver + oxygen

THERMAL ENERGY

■ Extraction of silver by thermal decomposition

Heating with carbon: extracting iron

Iron is the second most common metal in the Earth's crust, and is the metal most useful to humans. Fortunately, the metal is not very reactive. Most importantly, **iron is below carbon in the reactivity series**. The most common ore of iron is **hematite**, which is made up of iron oxide and sand. The iron oxide is reduced in a set of chemical reactions that depend on the presence of carbon. This process may be carried out on an enormous scale in a blast furnace.

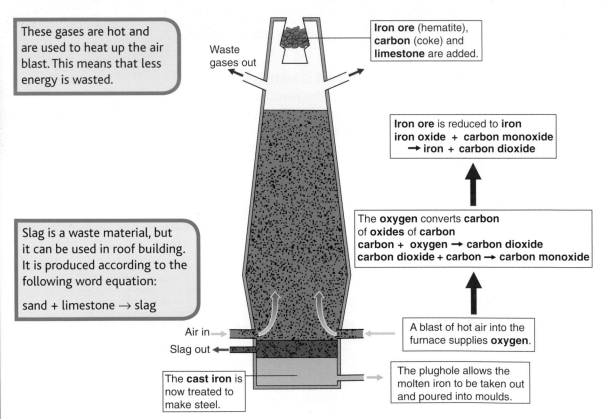

These gases are hot and are used to heat up the air blast. This means that less energy is wasted.

Waste gases out

Iron ore (hematite), **carbon** (coke) and **limestone** are added.

Iron ore is reduced to **iron**
iron oxide + carbon monoxide → iron + carbon dioxide

The **oxygen** converts **carbon** of **oxides** of **carbon**
carbon + oxygen → carbon dioxide
carbon dioxide + carbon → carbon monoxide

Slag is a waste material, but it can be used in roof building. It is produced according to the following word equation:

sand + limestone → slag

Air in

Slag out

The **cast iron** is now treated to make steel.

A blast of hot air into the furnace supplies **oxygen**.

The plughole allows the molten iron to be taken out and poured into moulds.

■ The reduction of iron ore in a blast furnace

The sand in the original ore makes the iron impure, which is why limestone is added to the furnace. The limestone reacts with silica (sand) to make a compound called calcium silicate. The molten calcium silicate, called **slag** in the steel industry, is skimmed off the top of the molten iron. This molten iron still contains about 4% carbon; it is called **cast iron** and is very brittle. Most industries need the iron to be less brittle and so the cast iron is converted to **steel**. Steel is made by removing most of the carbon and by adding small amounts of other elements. Stainless steel, for example, contains chromium and nickel as well as iron.

Exercise 8.3: Extraction of metals

1 Copy and complete this paragraph:

Some metals, such as _____ and silver, are found as the uncombined metal in nature. Most metals are found combined as _____ in _____ such as hematite and bauxite. There are three stages in the extraction of a metal: _____, _____ (which always involves some chemical reactions) and _____ (which makes the metal suitable for use).

2 Copy and complete this table.

Metal	Main ore	One important use of the metal	Method of extraction
Gold			
	Hematite		
		Wire for the conduction of electricity	
	Bauxite		
Mercury			

3 Write out word equations for each of the following chemical reactions:
   (a) the thermal decomposition of mercury oxide
   (b) the use of carbon to reduce tin oxide.

9 Acids, bases and indicators

You might already know something about **acids** from your Biology studies or from everyday life. For example:

- there is hydrochloric acid in your stomach that helps **enzymes** to digest proteins and kill micro-organisms
- many people enjoy the smell of ethanoic acid in vinegar on fish and chips.

Acids in everyday life: natural acids

We come across many examples of acids in our everyday lives. If you eat yoghurt, the slightly sour taste is because you are eating lactic acid (made from the sugar in milk). If you are bitten by an ant, the sting you feel is because the ant has injected methanoic acid under your skin. If you add vinegar to fish and chips, the vinegar is partly made of ethanoic acid. We don't just come across these acids by accident; they usually have a particular purpose.

- Acids often slow down the growth of micro-organisms and so can be used to preserve foods. Vinegar, for example, has been used for centuries to pickle foods, such as onions and cabbage.
- Ascorbic acid (vitamin C), found in foods such as oranges and lemons, helps to maintain healthy connective tissues and prevent scurvy. Ascorbic acid is also added to many foods because it prevents the oxidation of food molecules, a process that makes pungent and unpleasant smells.

Some of these natural acids are shown in the following table.

Name of acid	Where it is found
Ascorbic acid	In some fruits (like oranges) and vegetables (like potatoes)
Citric acid	Lemon juice
Ethanoic acid	Vinegar
Hydrochloric acid	Stomach juices
Lactic acid	Sour milk and yoghurt
Methanoic acid	Stings from ants and stinging nettles
Tannic acid	Tea

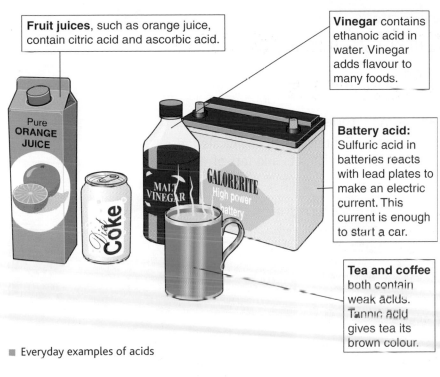

Fruit juices, such as orange juice, contain citric acid and ascorbic acid.

Vinegar contains ethanoic acid in water. Vinegar adds flavour to many foods.

Battery acid: Sulfuric acid in batteries reacts with lead plates to make an electric current. This current is enough to start a car.

Tea and coffee both contain weak acids. Tannic acid gives tea its brown colour.

Did you know?

Fizzy drinks contain dissolved carbon dioxide to make them fizzy. The dissolved gas makes a weak acid called carbonic acid. Acid and sugar in fizzy drinks are bad for your teeth!

■ Everyday examples of acids

Laboratory acids

Acids used in the laboratory are more **corrosive** than natural acids. This means that they can damage clothing, eyes or skin. Protective clothing and eyewear must be worn when working with acids. All containers of laboratory acids must have the warning symbol for corrosive on them (see right).

One material that is not corroded by acid is glass. This is why glass bottles are used for keeping and storing acids in the laboratory.

HAZARD!

In the laboratory **never** add water to an acid in a test tube or beaker. **Always** add acid to water. This is because some acids give out thermal energy when diluted. The water can boil and 'spit' into your face.

■ This symbol is part of the **Hazchem** system. These symbols tell us which chemicals are safe and which are dangerous. Remind yourself of the other hazard symbols by looking at the 'Investigations in science' section at the beginning of this book

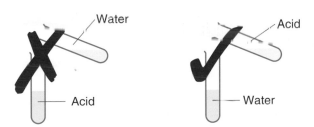

Water

Acid

Acid

Water

■ Remember: always add acid to water, not the other way round

Dealing with spills: in the laboratory

- Wash the affected area with a lot of water.
- **Tell the teacher.**
- Mop up the area, then wash it again with water.

Dealing with spills: on roads or in factories

Symbols on the lorry tell police and firefighters which chemicals the lorry is carrying. If it is acid, it is diluted with lots and lots of water.

■ The hazard symbol on this lorry shows that it is carrying corrosive material

■ The hazard symbol on this lorry shows that it is carrying flammable material

Uses of laboratory acids

The three common laboratory acids are hydrochloric acid, nitric acid and sulfuric acid. They are used in many chemical experiments and they also have important uses in industry.

■ Uses of the three common laboratory acids

Acid	Salts made in laboratory reactions	Important uses in industry
Hydrochloric acid (HCl)	Chlorides	In metal processing and purification of ores
Nitric acid	Nitrates	Making fertilisers and explosives
Sulfuric acid	Sulfates	Making fertilisers, paints and plastics; used in car batteries

Strong and weak acids

It is very important not to get mixed up between how **strong** an acid is and how **concentrated** it is.

- Strength is a chemical property of an acid. It tells us how easily the hydrogen in an acid combines with another substance. For example, a strong acid will react very quickly with a metal.
- Concentration is a physical property of the acid. It depends on how much water is present in the solution of the acid.

It is quite possible to have a dilute solution of a strong acid. For example, dilute nitric acid is a dilute solution of a strong acid; it is not very concentrated but still reacts quickly with metals. It is also possible to have a strong solution of a weak acid. Many metal cleaners are solutions of weak acids, like methanoic acid; these cleaners will remove the limescale from inside a kettle but will not attack the metal of the kettle itself.

If a large amount of an acid or an alkali is spilt, the fire brigade will often hose down the area with large volumes of water. The corrosive substance will become less concentrated. Dilute acids and alkalis are less hazardous than concentrated ones.

Bases and alkalis

There are so many different chemicals in the world that it is impossible to remember them all. What scientists like to do is to put chemicals into groups. All the chemicals in the same group have similar properties and this helps scientists to predict what they can be used for. Acids make up one of these groups, and bases and alkalis make up another.

- A base is a substance that can neutralise an acid. Metal oxides, carbonates and hydroxides are all examples of bases.
- An alkali is a base that can dissolve in water. The oxides of reactive metals, such as sodium and calcium, are alkalis. Hydroxides, such as ammonium hydroxide, sodium hydroxide and calcium hydroxide (limewater), are also alkalis.
- Alkalis can be strong or weak. Oxides and hydroxides of sodium and calcium are stronger than those of less reactive metals.

Bases and alkalis are the chemical opposite of acids.

Uses of alkalis

Alkalis can be just as corrosive as acids and can be very dangerous to humans. We say that these substances are **caustic**. We use many alkalis as cleaning materials.

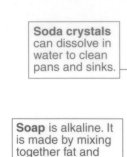

Soda crystals can dissolve in water to clean pans and sinks.

Oven cleaner sometimes contains very concentrated and very strong alkali. This reacts with fats and burned-on grease and makes them easier to dissolve in water.

Milk of magnesia neutralises stomach acid to overcome upset stomachs.

Soap is alkaline. It is made by mixing together fat and caustic soda (sodium hydroxide).

Toothpaste is an alkali that helps to whiten the teeth and neutralise acids from food.

HAZARD! Alkalis can be even more corrosive than acids. For this reason, gloves, overalls and eye protection should be worn when using oven cleaners and drain cleaners.

■ The importance of alkalis

Exercise 9.1: Acids and bases

1 Why does pickling food help to preserve it?

2 Give two uses of acids in industry.

3 What is an alkali? Give one important use of alkalis.

4 Copy and complete the paragraph, using words from the list below:

water, corrosive, goggles/eye protection, overalls/lab coat, acid

Acids and alkalis are _____, which means that they can cause damage to the skin. If one of these substances is spilt or splashed onto the skin, plenty of cold water must be run over the splashed area. In the laboratory, you should always add _____ to _____ and never the other way round. When working with acids or alkalis, you should always wear _____ and _____.

Extension questions

5 What is the benefit of having hydrochloric acid in your stomach? Why could this be harmful?

6 Ascorbic acid (vitamin C) is an antioxidant. Use the internet or your library to find out what an antioxidant does, and which kinds of food contain antioxidants.

◯ Acid or alkali: using indicators

Acids and alkalis are important chemicals but can be dangerous if they are not used properly. Acids have the opposite chemical properties to alkalis.

Strong acids and alkalis are corrosive and so could be very harmful to humans. Even so, there are many chemical and industrial reactions where we need to use these chemicals. How can we test for these chemicals without harming ourselves? You can find out if a substance is an acid or an alkali by using an **indicator**. An indicator contains a dye that changes colour depending on whether it is mixed with an acid or an alkali.

Plant dyes can be used as indicators

You can make an indicator from the dye in some coloured plants. Red cabbage, blackcurrant and raw beetroot are all suitable plants and the indicator can be obtained as shown in the following diagram.

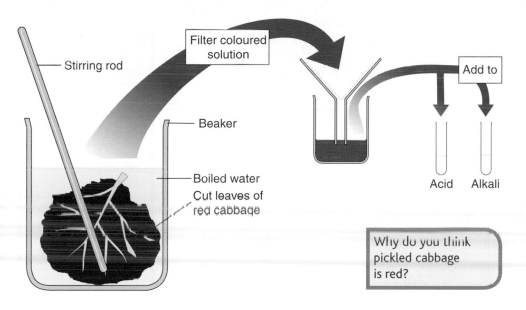

Why do you think pickled cabbage is red?

Solution	Red cabbage	Raw beetroot	Blackcurrant	Acid or alkali?
Sodium hydroxide	Green/yellow	Yellow	Green	Alkali
Hydrochloric acid	Pink/red	Red/purple	Red	Acid

Using litmus

An indicator that is often used in laboratories is called **litmus**. This can be used as a liquid or as papers that have been soaked in the liquid and then dried out. The colour changes for litmus with acid and alkali are shown in the following diagram.

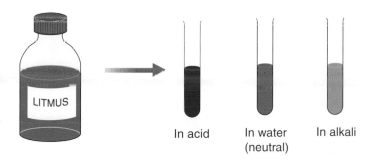

Two common acidic gases are carbon dioxide and sulfur dioxide.

Universal indicator and the pH scale

Litmus and plant dye indicators only tell us whether a substance is acid or alkaline. These indicators do not tell us how strongly acidic or alkaline the substance is. Some indicators can measure the strength of an acid or alkali and give us a numerical value on the pH scale. On this scale the values run from 0 to 14. Neutral substances have a pH value of 7, acid substances have a pH below 7 and alkaline substances have a pH value above 7.

One very useful indicator, which shows a range of colours, is **universal indicator** (or full-range indicator). This indicator can show whether a substance is acid or alkali and how strong it is.

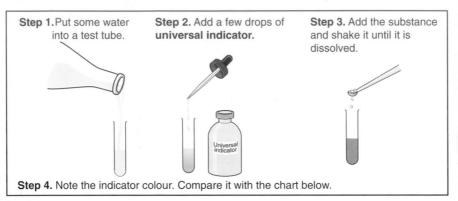

Step 1. Put some water into a test tube.

Step 2. Add a few drops of **universal indicator.**

Step 3. Add the substance and shake it until it is dissolved.

Step 4. Note the indicator colour. Compare it with the chart below.

■ Using universal indicator

Universal indicator has a whole range of colours from red through green to purple, as shown in the following diagram.

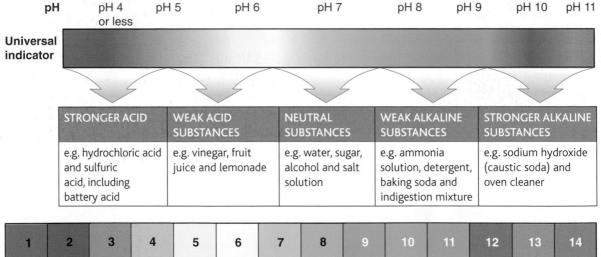

| pH | pH 4 or less | pH 5 | pH 6 | pH 7 | pH 8 | pH 9 | pH 10 | pH 11 |

STRONGER ACID	WEAK ACID SUBSTANCES	NEUTRAL SUBSTANCES	WEAK ALKALINE SUBSTANCES	STRONGER ALKALINE SUBSTANCES
e.g. hydrochloric acid and sulfuric acid, including battery acid	e.g. vinegar, fruit juice and lemonade	e.g. water, sugar, alcohol and salt solution	e.g. ammonia solution, detergent, baking soda and indigestion mixture	e.g. sodium hydroxide (caustic soda) and oven cleaner

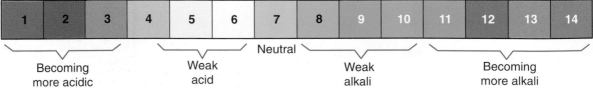

| 1 | 2 | 3 | 4 | 5 | 6 | 7 | 8 | 9 | 10 | 11 | 12 | 13 | 14 |

Becoming more acidic — Weak acid — Neutral — Weak alkali — Becoming more alkali

■ The pH scale (a scale of numbers ranging from 1 to 14)

Substances with very low or very high pH values are the most dangerous.

Investigation: Indicators

Litmus will only tell us whether a substance is an acid or an alkali. There are several other indicators – you are going to test two of them:

- Universal indicator, obtained from a chemical supplier.
- Red cabbage indicator, made in school from the leaves of red cabbage (see page 113).

Use a spotting tile to test the samples. You will need to add three drops of the indicator to each sample. **Make sure you organise this experiment carefully so that your tests do not get muddled.** Write the final colour of your results in a copy of the table below.

	Dilute HCl	Dilute NaOH	Lemon juice	Shampoo	Limewater	Tap water
Red cabbage						
Universal Indicator						

1 Which samples are acids and which are alkalis?
2 In what way is universal indicator more useful than litmus?

Neutralisation: reactions between acids and alkalis

When acids and alkalis are mixed, they cancel each other out. If the correct amounts are added to each other, a neutral solution can be formed. This kind of chemical reaction is called **neutralisation** and is a very common reaction in chemistry.

> Neutralisation is obtained by mixing equal quantities of acid and alkali of the same concentration.

Checking neutralisation with universal indicator

Universal indicator can be used to show a neutralisation taking place.

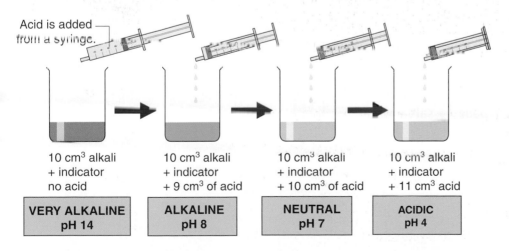

Acid is added from a syringe.

10 cm³ alkali + indicator no acid	10 cm³ alkali + indicator + 9 cm³ of acid	10 cm³ alkali + indicator + 10 cm³ of acid	10 cm³ alkali + indicator + 11 cm³ acid
VERY ALKALINE pH 14	**ALKALINE** pH 8	**NEUTRAL** pH 7	**ACIDIC** pH 4

The chemistry of neutralisation produces a salt and water.
There is a word equation for this type of reaction:

acid + base → salt + water

One example is:

hydrochloric acid + sodium hydroxide → sodium chloride + water

Universal indicator gives us the pH value as a whole number, but sometimes we could disagree about the exact value because we each see colours slightly differently. The pH scale actually has values between these whole numbers – there can be a pH of 4.2 or 9.3, for example. A **pH probe** can be used to measure the pH of a solution when an exact value is required.

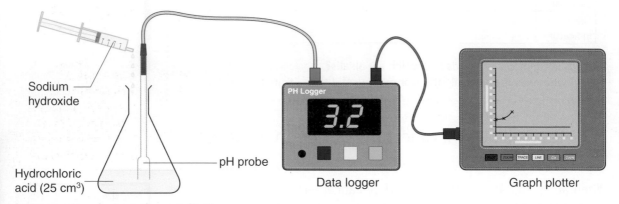

Sodium hydroxide

Hydrochloric acid (25 cm³)

pH probe

Data logger

Graph plotter

■ Using a pH probe to study neutralisation

Making salts

Neutralisation reactions are important because they can be used to make salts. Some of these salts are very useful chemicals, for example as fertilisers, weedkillers or drugs. It is important to measure the pH during neutralisation, because the acid needs to be neutralised exactly by the base. The diagram on the next page shows how a salt can be made using neutralisation.

Remember:

acid + base → salt + water

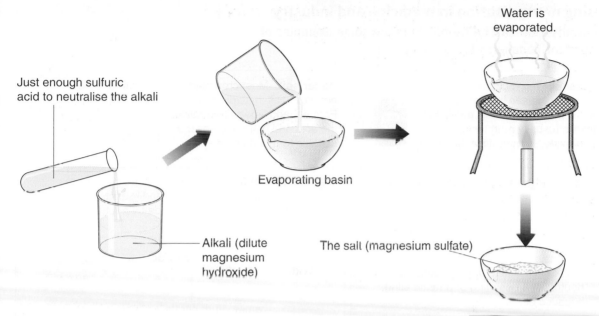

Just enough sulfuric acid to neutralise the alkali

Alkali (dilute magnesium hydroxide)

Evaporating basin

Water is evaporated.

The salt (magnesium sulfate)

Larger crystals are obtained if the solution is allowed to evaporate slowly, without extra heating.

Acids can be neutralised by insoluble bases as well as alkalis. For example, sulfuric acid is neutralised by copper oxide to form copper sulfate and water.

Salts can also be made in other chemical reactions involving acid (see 'Acids and metals' later in this chapter).

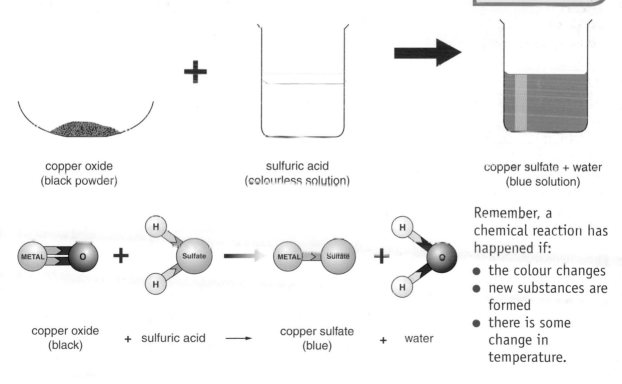

copper oxide (black powder)

sulfuric acid (colourless solution)

copper sulfate + water (blue solution)

copper oxide (black) + sulfuric acid ⟶ copper sulfate (blue) + water

Remember, a chemical reaction has happened if:
- the colour changes
- new substances are formed
- there is some change in temperature.

Using neutralisation in medicine and industry

Neutralisation can be useful. Here are some examples of important commercial neutralisations.

Antacid: Too much acid in the stomach causes indigestion. Medicines to ease this can contain alkalis (usually magnesium hydroxide) to neutralise the acid.

Better soil: Most crop plants do not grow well in acidic soils. Farmers add lime to neutralise the acid and make the soil more suitable for plant growth.

Dealing with stings: Wasps and bees give painful stings but they cannot be treated in the same way.

- A weak acid, like vinegar, can neutralise a wasp sting, because a wasp sting is alkaline.
- A weak alkali, like baking soda, can neutralise a bee sting or a nettle sting, because bee and nettle stings are acidic.

Manufacture of fertiliser: Plants need nitrogen to grow well. Farmers add nitrogen fertilisers to increase the soil fertility. Fertilisers can be made by neutralisation.

nitric acid + ammonium hydroxide
(acid)   (alkali)

↓

ammonium nitrate + water
(salt)   (water)
(fertiliser)

You may have heard, or even tried yourself, that rubbing a nettle sting with a dock leaf soothes the pain. This is a particularly handy treatment since nettle and dock commonly grow near each other. However, scientists have found that dock leaves are acidic and in fact their soothing affect comes from the moist, cooling sap, rather than a neutralisation reaction.

Did you know?

Most plants cannot absorb minerals in acidic soils. Carnivorous plants, such as sundew, obtain their nitrate from the bodies of insects they catch.

■ Sundew

If you want to send a secret note, you can use neutralisation. Here's how to do it:

- Write using a cotton bud dipped in a solution of baking soda (an alkali). It will be invisible when it dries.
- To show up the writing, paint over the paper with vinegar or grape juice (both are acids).
- The acid and the alkali react together to produce a coloured salt, so that the message can be read.

Exercise 9.2: Neutralisation

1 Nettle stings contain methanoic acid. What would you use on a nettle sting to make it less painful?

2 Aspirin solution turns universal indicator orange–red. What does this show?

3 This table lists the pH of several solutions:

Solution	A	B	C	D	E
pH	7	5	1	10	3

Name the solution or solutions that:

(a) would turn litmus blue
(b) would turn universal indicator orange or red
(c) is neither acidic nor alkaline
(d) could be used on a wasp sting.

Extension questions

4 You have four different antacid treatments (indigestion remedies). Describe how you would tell which one was most powerful. Include a list of the apparatus you would use and the steps you would take.

5 Dani and Noah carried out a neutralisation reaction. They slowly added sodium hydroxide to 25 cm³ of hydrochloric acid and used a pH probe to measure the pH of the solution. Here are their results:

Volume of sodium hydroxide added/cm³	0	5	10	20	25	30	40	50	60
pH	1	1	1.3	2.5	7	10	12.5	13	13

(a) Plot their results in a line graph.
(b) Try to explain the shape of the graph.
(c) How could they improve their results?

More reactions of acids

Remember that:

- some metals react with acids to produce a salt and hydrogen gas
- alkalis react with acids in a process called neutralisation to produce a salt and water.

Acids and metal carbonates

Metal carbonates are compounds that contain a metal and a **carbonate**. The carbonate is made up of carbon and oxygen. An acid always reacts with a carbonate by breaking it down to give off carbon dioxide gas. The carbon dioxide makes the mixture fizz (this fizzing is sometimes called **effervescence**) and will turn limewater milky. The following diagram shows how you can test that this is happening.

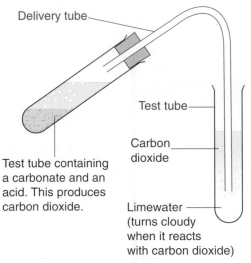

Delivery tube

Test tube

Carbon dioxide

Test tube containing a carbonate and an acid. This produces carbon dioxide.

Limewater (turns cloudy when it reacts with carbon dioxide)

■ Reaction of acids and carbonates

This reaction goes on for longer if the salt is soluble. For example, hydrochloric acid and calcium carbonate make calcium chloride. This salt dissolves away and lets the reaction carry on. Sulfuric acid and calcium carbonate, however, make calcium sulfate. This salt is insoluble and makes a layer around the calcium carbonate. This keeps the acid away from the carbonate and the reaction is stopped.

A good example is:

copper carbonate (green) + sulfuric acid ⟶ copper sulfate (blue) + water + carbon dioxide

The general word equation for this type of reaction is:

acid + metal carbonate → salt + water + carbon dioxide

You can see that a salt is formed, as well as the carbon dioxide. Remember that salts are very important chemicals, so this is another good method for the production of salts. Some real word equations for acids reacting with metal carbonates are:

nitric acid + lead carbonate → lead nitrate + water + carbon dioxide

hydrochloric acid + calcium carbonate → calcium chloride + water + carbon dioxide

Limestone contains the compound calcium carbonate. Rainwater contains weak acids and these react slowly with limestone and break it down. Buildings, pavements and statues made of limestone are attacked by rain and can be severely damaged over a long period of time. The problem is made worse if the rain becomes more acidic. Acid rain contains extra acids and so speeds up the breakdown of limestone rocks. The importance of these reactions with limestone is described in the following diagram.

Limestone

Marble

Limestone contains calcium carbonate (and so does marble).
Calcium carbonate reacts with the acids:

calcium + hydrochloric → calcium + water + carbon dioxide
carbonate   acid   chloride

This is very soluble and easily washed away – the limestone seems to disappear!

This fizzes and so is an excellent test to check whether a rock contains a carbonate.

Acid rain damages buildings made of limestone and makes underground caves in areas of limestone rock.

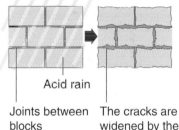

Acid rain

Joints between blocks

The cracks are widened by the acid rain.

■ Reaction of limestone with acid

Acids and metals

Acids react with metals to produce salts and hydrogen gas.
For example:

zinc + sulfuric acid → zinc sulfate + hydrogen

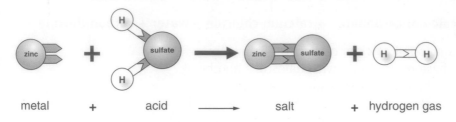

metal　　　+　　　acid　　　──────→　　　salt　　　+　hydrogen gas

Summary of acid reactions

Acids are very important chemicals. We have spent a lot of time looking at their properties and their reactions. There is a lot to learn, so here is a useful summary of these properties and reactions.

Remind yourself!

Test for hydrogen: the **squeaky pop**.

Test for carbon dioxide: the **milky limewater**.

Did you know?

Bacteria in your mouth feed on sugar and create acids. These acids can cause tooth decay.

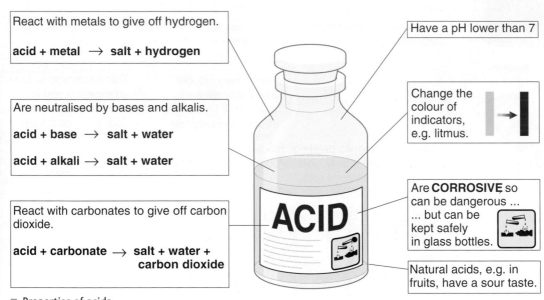

React with metals to give off hydrogen.

acid + metal → salt + hydrogen

Are neutralised by bases and alkalis.

acid + base → salt + water

acid + alkali → salt + water

React with carbonates to give off carbon dioxide.

acid + carbonate → salt + water + carbon dioxide

Have a pH lower than 7

Change the colour of indicators, e.g. litmus.

Are **CORROSIVE**, so can be dangerous …
… but can be kept safely in glass bottles.

Natural acids, e.g. in fruits, have a sour taste.

■ Properties of acids

Exercise 9.3: More reactions of acids

1 Copy and complete the following word equations:
   (a) zinc + _____ → zinc chloride + hydrogen
   (b) nitric acid + magnesium → _____ + _____
   (c) _____ + potassium hydroxide → potassium sulfate + _____
   (d) copper carbonate + hydrochloric acid → _____ + _____ +

   _____

   (e) lead + _____ → lead sulfate + _____

2 Which acid and base would you use to produce the following salts?
   (a) copper chloride   (c) iron chloride
   (b) lead nitrate   (d) zinc sulfate

3 Why is acid kept in glass bottles and not in metal containers?

4 Read this passage and answer the questions that follow:

   When an excess of calcium carbonate is added to dilute hydrochloric acid, a chemical reaction occurs. Some of the powder dissolves and a gas is given off. Once the reaction is finished, the excess calcium carbonate can be filtered off. The salt formed can be obtained by evaporation of the filtrate.

   (a) How can you tell that this is a chemical change?
   (b) What is the name of the gas given off? How can you test for this gas?
   (c) How can you tell when the reaction is finished?
   (d) What is the name of the salt formed during the reaction?
   (e) How could you make sure that you obtained large crystals of this salt?

5 Copy and complete this paragraph, using words from the list below:

   carbonates, hydrogen, salt, (squeaky) pop, calcium carbonate

   Acids react with most metals to produce a _____ and a gas called
   _____. This gas makes a _____ when tested with a lighted splint.
   Acids react with _____ to make a salt, water and carbon dioxide gas.
   Limestone contains the compound _____, which can be dissolved by
   acid in rainwater.

Extension questions

6 A well-known recipe for making blackcurrant and apple jam recommends
   that the fruit is boiled in a copper pan and not in an iron pan. Can you
   explain this?

7 Jenny and her friend Charles were interested in the reaction between
   marble chips and dilute hydrochloric acid. They added 20 g of large marble
   chips to 50 cm³ of dilute hydrochloric acid in a large conical flask, as shown
   in the diagram on the next page.

Working Scientifically

123

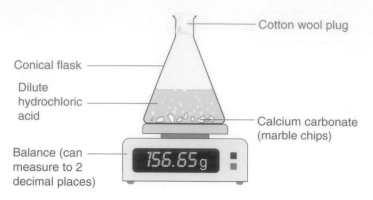

Cotton wool plug

Conical flask

Dilute hydrochloric acid

Calcium carbonate (marble chips)

Balance (can measure to 2 decimal places)

156.65 g

The decrease in mass during the experiment is noted at one minute intervals.

calcium carbonate + hydrochloric acid → calcium chloride + carbon dioxide + water

They measured the loss in mass every minute for ten minutes. This was their first experiment. Jenny and Charles then repeated the experiment, but this time they crushed the 20 g of marble into very small pieces before they added it to the hydrochloric acid. This was their second experiment. The results of their experiments are shown in the table.

Time/minutes	First experiment (large chips): loss of mass, in grams	Second experiment (crushed chips): loss of mass, in grams
1	1.10	2.15
2	1.90	3.05
3	2.50	3.45
4	2.95	3.65
5	3.20	3.70
6	3.40	3.70
7	3.50	3.70
8	3.60	3.70
9	3.70	3.70
10	3.70	3.70

(a) Plot a graph of these results. Put time on the *x*-axis (bottom) and loss in mass on the *y*-axis (side).
(b) Which experiment goes the fastest at the start of the reaction?
(c) Why do both of the graphs eventually become horizontal?
(d) What do the results tell you about the effect of surface area on the rate of a chemical reaction?

Glossary

Acid   a substance that can give up hydrogen in a chemical reaction and always has a pH less than 7.

Acid rain   happens when oxides made in combustion combine with water vapour in the air.

Alkali   a base that is soluble in water and always has a pH more than 7.

Apparatus   the equipment used for scientific experiments.

Atom   the basic unit that makes up an element.

Base   (of chemicals) a substance that can neutralise an acid.

Brownian motion   the random movement of particles in a liquid or a gas.

Carbonate   a compound that contains a metal, carbon and oxygen, and always gives off carbon dioxide when it reacts with an acid

Change of state   the conversion of a substance from one form to another.

Chemical bond   a link that forms between elements.

Chemical change (or reaction)   a reaction that results in new products and an energy change and that is very difficult to reverse.

Chemical formula   a shorthand version of the name for a compound, written using chemical symbols. The formula for an element tells you whether it is made of single atoms or a molecule.

Chemical symbol   the one- or two-letter symbol given to an element. For example calcium is Ca.

Chromatography   separation of dissolved materials depending on how well they are carried through a special kind of paper by a moving solvent.

Combustion   a chemical reaction that involves a substance (fuel) burning in oxygen and giving out thermal energy.

Compound   a chemical substance made of different elements linked to one another.

Concentration   how many particles of a substance there are mixed with a certain number of particles of water.

Condensation   the change of state from gas (vapour) to liquid, speeded up by cooling.

Conductor   a material that is good at transferring thermal or electrical energy.

Conservation of mass   during any physical or chemical change the total mass of the reactants used is the same as the total mass of the products formed.

Corrosion   damage to a metal caused by a chemical reaction (oxidation) between the metal and oxygen in the air without any burning.

Corrosive   able to attack other materials, including skin.

Decanting   separation of a solid from a liquid by careful pouring.

Decomposition   a chemical reaction in which one substance is broken down into several products.

Diffusion   the random movement of particles down a gradient of concentration.

Displacement reaction   a reaction in which one element replaces another one in a compound.

Distillation   the process of separation that depends on substances in a solution or mixture having different boiling points.

Element   a substance made of only one type of atom.

Enzyme   a protein that is a catalyst in a biological system.

Evaporation   the change of state from liquid to gas (vapour), speeded up by heating.

Filter   a layer with many tiny holes that let liquid through but keep back the solids.

Filtrate   the liquid that has passed through a filter.

Filtration   the process of separation that uses a filter to separate a solid from a liquid.

Fractional distillation   the technique for separating liquids in a mixture due to their boiling points, using a fractionating column.

Fuel   a substance that can be burned to release energy.

Galvanising   protection of a metal by coating it with zinc.

Global warming   the raising of the Earth's temperature as a result of pollution and the greenhouse effect.

Greenhouse effect   the trapping of thermal (internal) energy close to the Earth by a layer of gases.

Indicator   a substance that changes colour according to the pH of another substance.

Insoluble   a substance that is unable to dissolve in a solvent.

Lime   a compound made when limestone is crushed and heated strongly.

Metal   an element on the left of the Periodic Table that usually conducts thermal energy and electricity.

Mixture   a substance that contains more than one type of particle, not chemically linked to one another.

Molecule   two or more atoms joined together.

Neutral   a solution that is neither acid nor alkaline and has a pH of 7.

Neutralisation   a chemical reaction between an acid and an alkali or base.

Non-metal   an element on the right of the Periodic Table that usually does not conduct thermal energy or electricity.

Ore   a rock that contains a metal.

Oxidation   a chemical reaction in which an element is combined with oxygen.

Oxide   a compound formed when an element combines with oxygen.

Periodic Table   a chart that arranges all the elements in order of their atomic number and in groups and periods according to their properties.

pH scale   a scale of numbers, from 0–14, that gives a measurement of acidity or alkalinity.

Physical change   a change in the way a material looks or feels. It involves no new products and can be reversed.

Product   the material present after a chemical change has taken place.

Property   any characteristic of a substance, such as colour, compressibility or shape.

Pure   describes a substance that is made of only one type of particle.

Reactant   the starting material in a chemical change.

Reactive   will easily take part in a chemical reaction.

Reactivity series   metals listed in order of how easily they take part in chemical reactions.

Reduction   a chemical reaction in which substances lose oxygen or gain hydrogen.

Residue   the solid that is kept back by a filter.

Rusting   the corrosion of iron and steel.

Salt   one product of the neutralisation reaction between an acid and a base.

Saturated   a solution made when the maximum amount of a solute that can dissolve has been added to a solvent.

Sediment   the insoluble material that settles to the bottom of a container of solvent.

Soluble   a substance that will dissolve in a solvent.

Solubility   a measure of the amount of a substance that will dissolve in a certain volume of a solvent at a particular temperature.

Solute   the substance that dissolves in a solvent when a solution is made.

Solution   a mixture of a solute in a solvent.

Solvent   the liquid that dissolves a solute.

States of matter   the forms in which a substance can exist, as solid, liquid or gas.

Strength   (of chemicals) how easily an acid or alkali reacts with other substances.

Suspension   a mixture made of a liquid and an insoluble substance.

Variable   something (a factor) that changes during the course of an experiment.

Word equation   a scientific way of writing out in words what happens during a chemical change.

Index

Index